Belgium

a View from the Sky

Wim Robberechts

Belgium

a View from the Sky

davidsfonds.com

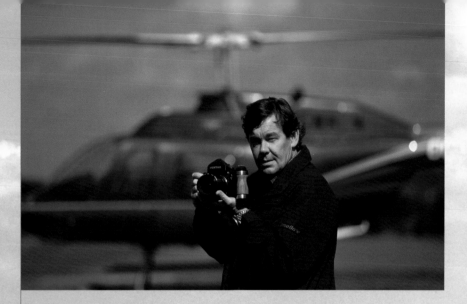

Woord vooraf

Wim Robberechts (Vilvoorde 1950) is gepokt en gemazeld door het televisie- en videotijdperk. De man die zich nu voorhoudt een prachtig beroep te hebben waar hij nooit op uitgekeken raakt – omdat het hem in staat stelt altijd iets anders en toch hetzelfde te doen – heeft er een kwarteeuw professionele carrière op zitten.

Robberechts is in de vroege jaren zeventig begonnen als cameraman, onder andere voor de toenmalige BRT. Hij waagde zich midden in de jaren tachtig heel even aan de Belgische videoclip ('Die heb ik mee uitgevonden'), maakte films en was een van de eersten om hier de mogelijkheden van de Steadicam uit te proberen. In 1984 stichtte hij zijn eigen productiebedrijf, Wim Robberechts & Co. Naast het verhuren van cameraploegen en de allermodernste montagefaciliteiten, heeft dat bedrijf zich gespecialiseerd in het maken van stabiele luchtopnamen. Met behulp van hun gyrogestabiliseerde cameraplatform, is er steeds een ploeg van Wim Robberechts & Co ergens in Europa actief.

Twee jaar geleden rijpte het plan om, na het spelen met zoveel technisch vernuft, even terug te grijpen naar de volkomen eenvoud van de fotografie: het diafragma instellen, de sluitertijd vastleggen, het beeld kaderen en… afdrukken.

'Pas op,' hoor ik de professional zeggen, 'ik ben geen beroepsfotograaf.' Het klinkt meer als een manifest dan als een verontschuldiging. Vrij vertaald: 'Mag ik even iets allereenvoudigst doen en er plezier aan beleven?'

Toch is hij na 25 jaar beroepsernst niet aan een of andere spielerei toe. Wim Robberechts heeft nooit zomaar iets gedaan. Niet dat er berekening mee gemoeid is, maar hij blijft ook in zijn meest poëtische momenten een vakman: de vastlegger van vluchtige momenten.

Wat hij aflevert is gaaf werk, altijd zo geweest. Niet zelden merkte de journalist die hem inhuurde bij de montage, dat zijn reportage veel te danken had aan wat het oog van Robberechts had vastgelegd. Zoals je nu bij het bekijken van zijn luchtfoto's moet toegeven dat hij ook hier – letterlijk en figuurlijk – in de diepte heeft gewerkt en een merkwaardig surplus levert, een derde dimensie: het reliëf.

Robberechts zal allicht zeggen dat hij gewoon de kansen van de luchtfotografie benut, maar hij heeft dat oog, dat precies ziet wat het vastlegt en weet hoe dat op papier zal komen. Hij is zijn vak begonnen in het prevideotijdperk, toen de cameraman al eens op zijn intuïtie moest vertrouwen omdat er met te ontwikkelen film en zonder al te gesofisticeerde apparatuur gewerkt werd.

Voor de foto's in dit boek heeft hij die ambachtelijke kwaliteit en het vermogen tot scheppen van enige meerwaarde ten volle benut.

Hij mag nu zelf zijn verhaal vertellen en het beeld meer dan ooit laten spreken. Robberechts heeft zich daarboven in zijn helikopter uitgeleefd in een passie, maar dan weer niet zonder dicht bij zijn vakkennis te blijven. De cameraman koos precies een fototoestel uit – opzettelijk niet het meest gesofisticeerde – waarmee hij op televisieformaat kon *framen*.

Hij koestert het resultaat. Voor één keer niet het bewegend beeld, maar dat bevroren moment dat op 1/125 seconde sluitertijd wordt vastgelegd: 'Zoveel tastbaarder, blijvender en beklijvender', hoor ik hem zeggen. Als dat geen liefdesverklaring is.

Avant-propos

Wim Robberechts (né à Vilvorde en 1950) est un vieux briscard de la télévision et de la vidéo. L'homme qui affirme faire un métier merveilleux dont il ne se lasse jamais – parce qu'il lui permet à chaque fois de faire autre chose, tout en restant le même – a déjà un quart de siècle d'activité professionnelle à son actif.

Robberechts a commencé comme cadreur au début des années 70, notamment pour la BRT. Au milieu des années 80, il a fait une incursion dans le monde du vidéoclip belge ("J'ai contribué à l'inventer), a réalisé des films et a été l'un des premiers dans ce pays à s'intéresser aux possibilités du Steadicam. En 1984, il a fondé sa propre maison de production, Wim Robberechts & Co. Outre la location d'équipes caméra et de facilités de montage ultramodernes, cette société s'est spécialisée dans les prises de vues aériennes stabilisées. Travaillant avec leurs plate-formes gyrostabilisées, les équipes de Wim Robberechts & Co, sont actives à travers toute l'Europe.

Il y a deux ans, l'idée lui est venue de laisser de côté la haute technologie, pour quelques heures au petit matin, et de retourner à l'absolue simplicité de la photographie: régler le diaphragme, déterminer le temps d' exposition, cadrer et … appuyer. J'entends le professionnel affirmer: "Attention, je ne suis pas photographe de métier". Mais ça ressemble plus à une profession de foi qu'à une excuse. Librement traduit, cela devient: "Me permettez-vous, pendant quelques instants, de passer à une activité extrêmement simple et d'y prendre plaisir?"

Toutefois, il ne va pas balayer vingt-cinq ans de probité professionnelle en s'amusant gratuitement. Wim Robberechts n'a jamais rien fait au hasard. Non pas qu'il agisse par calcul; tout simplement, même à ses moments les plus poétiques, il reste un professionel, l'archiveur d'instants fugaces.

Le travail qu'il fournit est soigné, comme cela a toujours été le cas. A maintes reprises, les journalistes qui avaient fait appel à ses services ont constaté au montage combien leur reportage devait au coup d'oeil de Robberechts. Ici, c'est pareil: en regardant ses photos aériennes, on reconnaît qu'il a travaillé en profondeur – au propre comme au figuré – et qu'il apporte aux images une remarquable plus-value, une troisième dimension, un relief.

Robberechts dira sans doute qu'il n' a fait qu'exploiter les possibilités de la photographie aérienne; mais son oeil voit avec une grande acuité tout ce qu'il enregistre et sait comment cela apparaîtra sur le papier. Il a démarré dans le métier à l'époque d'avant la vidéo, lorsqu'un cadreur devait souvent se fier à son intuition, car on se servait encore de pellicule à développer et d'équipements peu sophistiqués.

Pour la réalisation des photos qui suivent – qu'elles soient paisibles ou plus intenses – il a exploité à fond ce côté artisanal et son aptitude à créer une plus-value.

Laissons-le maintenant raconter son histoire, en donnant plus que jamais la parole à l'image.

Là-haut, dans son hélicoptère, Robberechts s'est livré à sa passion, sans pour autant renoncer à ses connaissances professionnelles. En bon caméraman, il a donné la préférence à un appareil photo lui permettant de cadrer au même format que la télévision – mais en optant délibérément pour un modèle simple.

Il chérit le résultat. Pour une fois, ce ne sont pas des images animées, mais un instant figé, enregistré avec un temps d'exposition de 1/125e seconde: "Tellement plus tangible, durable et persistant", me dit-il. N'est-ce pas là une déclaration d' amour?

Foreword

Wim Robberechts (Vilvoorde, 1950) is an old hand in the television and video business. He says he has a fabulous job of which he never tires, because it always lets him do something different while remaining essentially the same. It is a job he has now pursued for a quarter of century.

Robberechts began his career as a cameraman in the early 1970s, working for the BRT and other broadcasters. In the mid-1980s, he chanced his arm with a Belgian pop video ('I helped invent them'), made films and was one of the first to explore the potential of the Steadicam. In 1984, he founded his own production-company, Wim Robberechts & Co. Next to the location of camera crews and hyper-modern editing facilities, this company specialized in aerial cinematography. With their gyrostabilized camera-platforms, the crews of Wim Robberechts & Co are active all over Europe.

Two years ago, after playing with all these technical gadgets, he hatched a plan to return to the total simplicity of photography: setting the aperture, choosing the shutter-speed, framing the picture and shooting. "Mind you," says the professional, "I'm not a professional photographer." It sounds more like a manifesto than an apology. Freely translated, what he's saying is: "Can't I just do something simple for once and enjoy myself?"

For the past 25 years, in fact, he has always been seriously fooling around with something. Wim Robberechts never just does anything. Not that he is calculating, it's simply that the remains a craftsman, even in his most poetic moments, capturing the fleeting instant.

The work he produces is fabulous, as it always has been. Many of the journalists who have used his services have noticed during the editing stage that their final reports owed a lot to what Robberechts' eye had captured. Looking here at his aerial photographs, you have to admit that once again his work has great depth – both literal and figurative – and that it boasts that remarkable third dimension called relief.

Robberechts himself would probably say he just took advantage of the opportunities aerial photography has to offer. But he has the kind of eye that sees precisely what is being recorded and he knows how it will look on paper. He began his craft in the pre-video era, when cameramen frequently had to trust their intuition because they were working with film that had to be developed and were not using overly sophisticated equipment. In shooting the photographs for this book, he made full use of these craftsman's skills and his ability to create added value.

It's up to him now to tell his story and, more than ever, to let the images speak.

Robberechts was indulging a passion up there in his helicopter, but he never strayed far from his solid professional knowledge. The cameraman carefully chose a camera – deliberately not the most sophisticated – which allowed him to frame his shots with a TV aspect ratio. He cherishes the result. Just for once, it is not the moving image, but the frozen istant, captured at a shutter-speed of 1/125th of a second. "It's so much more tangible and lasting," I hear him say. A noble explanation if ever there was one.

Vorwort

Wim Robberechts (Jahrgang 1950) ist ein Kind des Fernseh- und Videozeitalters. Einen wunderschönen, endlos faszinierenden Beruf habe er, der es ihm ermögliche, immer weider etwas Neues und dabei doch immer das Gleiche zu tun. Ein Vierteljahrhundert Berufserfahrung hat er inzwischen auf dem Buckel.

Robberechts fing in den frühen Siebzigern als Kameramann an, unter anderem für das belgische Fernsehen, damals noch BRT. Er versuchte sich Mitte der achtziger Jahre am belgischen Videoclip ("Den habe ich ja mit erfunden"), drehte Kinofilme und war hierzulande einer der Ersten, die die Möglichkeiten der "Steadicam" ausprobierten. 1984 gründete er seinen eigenen Produktionsbetrieb, Wim Robberechts & Co. Neben der Vermietung modernster Schnittanlagen und kompletter Kamerateams, hat sich die Firma auf die Produktion von stabilen Luftaufnahmen spezialisiert. Fast täglich ist, irgendwo in Europa, ein Team von Wim Robberechts & Co. mit einer gyrostabilisierten Kamera in der Luft.

Vor zwei Jahren hatte er, nach all der raffinierten Spitzentechnologie, das Bedürfnis, zur vollkommenen Schlichtheit der Fotografie zurückkehren: Blende einstellen, Belichtungszeit festlegen, Ausschnitt bestimmen – auslösen. "Moment", sagt er, ganz und gar Profi, "Ich bin kein Berufsfotograf!" Es klingt eher nach einem Manifest als nach einer Entschuldiging. Frei übersetzt: "Darf ich denn bitte einmal ganz kurz etwas ganz Einfaches machen, nur aus Spaß an der Freud'?" Trotzdem geht es nicht nur um irgendeine kleine Spielerei, die er sich nach langjährigem Berufsernst einmal gönnen will. "Einfach nur so" hat Wim Robberecht noch nie etwas gemacht. Nicht, daß etwa Berechnung im Spiel wäre. Doch auch im verträumsten Moment bleibt er der nüchterne Fachmann, der den flüchtigen Augenblick festfalten will.

Was er abliefert, is solide Arbeit, immer schon. Manch ein Fernsehredakteur, der mit ihm gedreht hatte, stellte erst am Schneidetisch fest, wieviel sein Bericht dem Auge von Wim Robberechts zu verdanken hat. Auch seine Luftaufnahmen zeigen Tiefe, in beiden Bedeutungen des Wortes. Und einen merkwürdigen Mehrwert, eine dritte Dimension: das Relief.

Robberechts wird wohl behaupten, er habe lediglich die Möglichkeiten der Luftfotografie genutzt. Aber er hat nun einmal dieses Auge, das genau sieht, was es da fixiert, und wie nachher der Abzug ausschen wird. Sein Handwerk hat er in der Prä-Video-Ära gelernt. Damals mußte ein Kameramnn sich schon mal auf seine Intuition verlassen, denn man arbeitete ohne technische Sperenzchen und auf Film, der noch entwickelt werden mußte.

Für die Fotos in diesem Band hat er dieses handwerkliche Können und sein Vermögen, Mehrwert zu schöpfen, voll zur Geltung gebracht. Er darf jetzt selber seine Geschichte erzählen, das Bild, mehr denn je, sprechen lassen. Robberechts hat da oben, in seinem Hubschrauber, einer Leidenschaft gefrönt, dabei aber nie sein Handwerk vergessen. Miet Absicht suchte der Kameramann sich eine relativ schlichte Fotokamera aus, deren Ausschnitt dem Fernseh-Format entspricht. Mit dem Ergebnis ist er nicht unzufrieden: ausnahmsweise einmal kein bewegtes Bild, sondern nur den einen, eingefrorenen Moment, in 1/125 Sekunde Belichtungszeit festgehalten. "So viel greifbarer, bleibender, beständiger", hört man ihn sagen. Wenn das kleine Liebeserklärung ist…

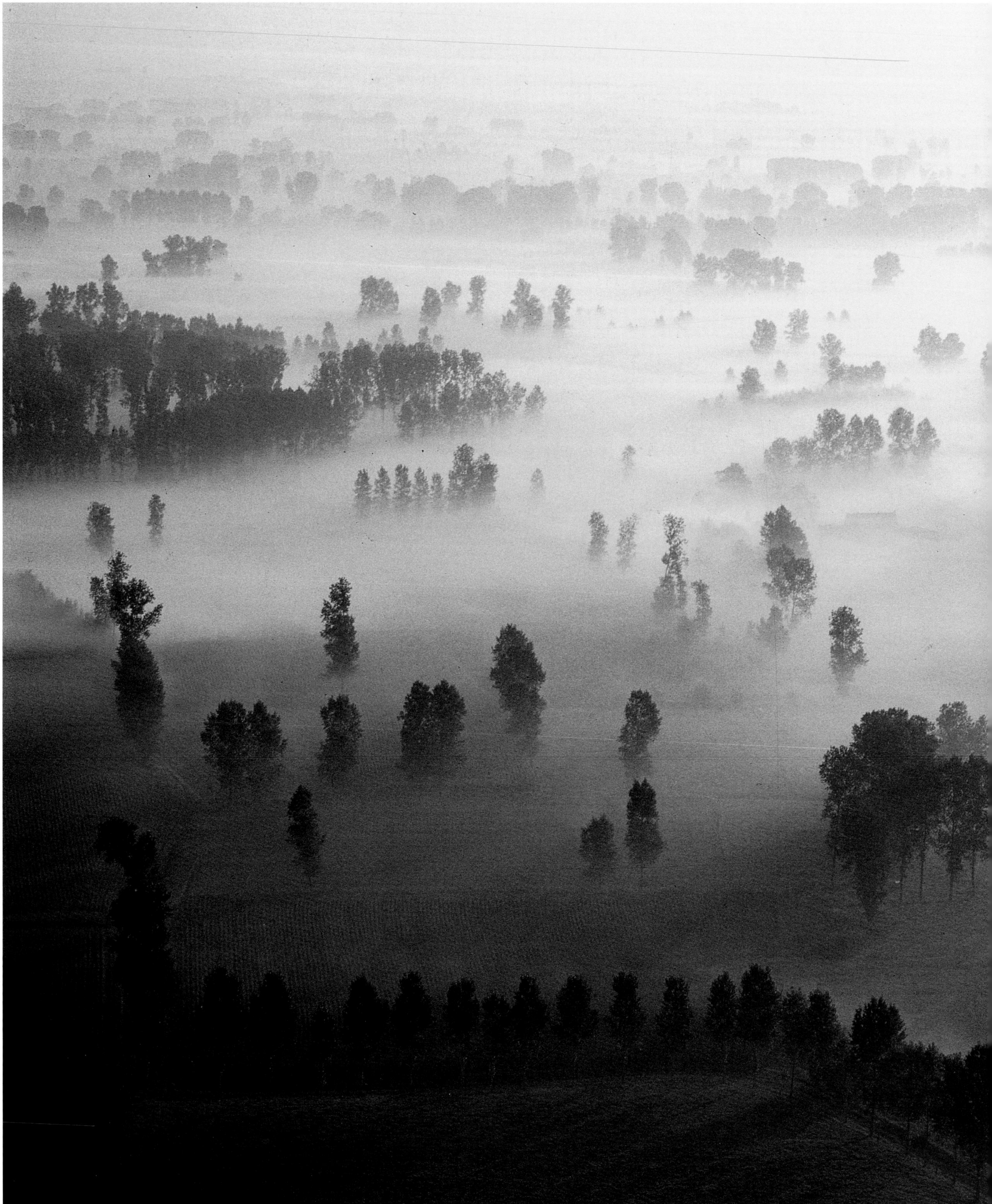

Bornem is een uitgestrekte gemeente aan de oevers van de Schelde, in het hart van Klein-Brabant. Het rivierenland is samengesteld uit bossen, polders, watervlaktes en dijken, wat het tot een uniek wandel- en natuurgebied maakt.

Bornem is a large village on the banks of the Scheldt in the heart of 'Little Brabant'. The river landscape consists of woods, polders, stretches of water and dikes, making it a unique area for walking and nature.

Bornem est une commune étendue sur les rives de l'Escaut, au coeur du Petit-Brabant. Ce pays de rivières comprend des bois, des polders, des plans d'eau et des digues, qui en font un domaine naturel unique et propice aux promenades.

Bornem ist eine ausgedehnte Gemeinde am Schelde-Ufer, im Herzen von 'Kleinbrabant'. Die Flußlandschaft aus Wäldern, Poldern, Wasserflächen und Deichen macht Bornem zu einem einmaligen Erholungsgebiet.

In de buurt van Sint-Truiden, midden het Haspengouwse plateau, staan de fruitbomen half april al in bloei. De aanblik van de vele boomgaarden is feeëriek.

In the neighbourhood of Sint-Truiden, in the centre of the plateau of Haspengouw, the fruit trees already blossom in the middle of the month of April. The sight of many orchards is quite enchanting.

Dans les environs de Saint-Trond, au centre du plateau hesbignon, les arbres fruitiers fleurissent déjà à la mi-avril. Assurément, la vue des nombreux vergers est féerique.

In der Gegend von Sint-Truiden, mitten in der Haspengouw-Hochebene, stehen die Obstbäume schon Mitte April in der Blüte. Die vielen Obstgärten bieten ganz sicher einen märchenhaften Anblick.

Het duinreservaat *de Westhoek* in De Panne is met zijn 120 hectaren duintoppen en -pannen het grootste beschermde duingebied van de hele kust. Het heeft een unieke flora en door de wind verandert het landschap voortdurend.

The dune reserve *the Westhoek*, in De Panne, with its 120 hectares of dune crests and valleys, is the largest protected dune area of the whole coast. The unique flora forms part of a landscape which is constantly changing due to the winds.

La réserve naturelle constituée de dunes *le Westhoek* à La Panne avec ses 120 hectares de collines de sable et de 'pannen' (dépressions dans les dunes) est le plus grand domaine protégé de dunes de toute la côte. Cette réserve naturelle possède une flore unique et le vent en modifie sans cesse le paysage.

Das Dünenreservat *von Westhoek* in De Panne ist mit seinen 120 Hektar Dünengipfeln und Dünenpfannen das größte geschützte Dünengebiet der gesamten Küste. Es besitzt eine einzigartige Flora und durch den Wind verändert sich die Landschaft ständig.

De Onze-Lieve-Vrouwe-kathedraal in Antwerpen is het hoogste bouwwerk van de Nederlanden. Ze ontleent haar schoonheid aan haar ranke en gotische pracht.

La cathédrale Notre-Dame d'Anvers est le bâtiment le plus haut des anciens Pays-Bas espagnols. Elle doit sa beauté à la magnificence élancée du gothique.

Our Lady's Cathedral in Antwerp is the highest historical building in the Low Countries. It derives its beauty from its slender Gothic splendour.

Die Liebfrauenkathedrale von Antwerpen - das höchste Gebäude der damaligen Niederlande. Schönheit durch ranke Gotik.

De Grote Markt van Brugge met het belfort. Deze stad was in de vroege Middel-eeuwen een van de belang-rijkste steden in Europa. Door de eeuwen heen behield ze haar middeleeuwse stratenpatroon. Thans is Brugge een druk toeristisch centrum.

La Grand-Place de Bruges et le beffroi. Cette ville était l'une des plus importantes d'Europe au début du Moyen-Age. Au fil des siècles, elle a conservé son plan de rues médiéval. De nos jours, Bruges est un centre touris-tique extrèmement couru.

The market square at Bruges, with its belfry tower. The city was one of Europe's most important cities in the Middle Ages. It has retained its medieval street-plan over the centuries and is nowadays a busy tourist centre.

Der Marktplatz von Brügge mit dem Bergfried. Im frühen Mittelalter war Brügge eine der wichtigsten Städte Europas. Die Stadt, die jahrhundertelang ihr altes Straßenmuster zu schützen wußte, ist heute ein touristisches Zentrum.

Een typisch Brabantse hoeve in de buurt van Tienen. Opmerkelijk is het gesloten vierkante grondplan. De Frankische U-vormige hoeve werd later gesloten tot een vierkant met een muur en een poortgebouw.

A typical Brabantine cottage in the neighbourhood of Tienen. The closed square ground plan is remarkable. The Frankish U-shaped cottage was lateron closed into a square, with the building of a wall and a gateway.

Une ferme brabançonne typique dans les environs de Tirlemont. Le plan carré fermé est remarquable: il s'agit d'une variante du type de fermes franc en forme de U, clôturé par la suite par un mur et un bâtiment abritant le portail.

Einen typisch Brabanter Bauernhof in der Gegend von Tienen. Auffällig ist der quadratische Grundriß, eine Variation des fränkischen Hoftyps mit der U-Form, der danach mit einer Mauer und einem Torgebäude geschlossen wurde.

Het Brabantse trekpaard is een koelbloedig dier dat het harde werk van de boer op het platteland moest verlichten. Vandaag is dat zware werkpaard een symbool voor de kracht en de tradities van Brabant.

Le cheval de trait brabançon est un animal impassible qui allégeait le travail du paysan. De nos jours, ce cheval massif symbolise la force et les traditions du Brabant.

The Brabantine draught horse used to work stoically for local farmers. This heavy working animal nowadays serves as a symbol of Brabant's strengths and traditions.

Der belgische Kaltblüter - das treue Zugpferd, das dem Bauern die Knochenarbeit erleichterte. Heute ist das Arbeitstier Wahrzeichen für brabanter Kraft und Tradition.

In Bokrijk wordt het verre verleden weer opgebouwd. Iedereen kan de huizen en de hoeven uit de tijd van de bokkenrijders bezichtigen. De legende wil dat rovers, gezeten op bokken, door de lucht kliefden.

A Bokrijk, le passé lointain a été reconstitué. Chacun peut y visiter les maisons et les fermes telles qu'elles étaient à l'époque des 'bokkenrijders' (la légende veut que des brigands, y fendaient l'air, montés sur des boucs).

The distant past has been reconstructed at Bokrijk. Visitors can explore houses and farms from the days of the 'Goat Riders'. Then according to legend, robbers mounted on goats flew through the air. ('Bokrijk' literally means 'Goat's Realm')

In Bokrijk wurde die Vergangenheit wiederhergestellt. Im Freilichtmuseum sind Häuser und Bauernhöfe aus der Zeit der 'Bockritter' zu besichtigen. Der Sage nach sollen die Räuber auf Böcken durch die Luft gebraust sein.

De *wind*molen van Onze-Lieve-Vrouw-Lombeek op een kruispunt van de tijd. *Graan-molens* waren een symbool voor de welvaart van het platteland. Na de industriële revolutie verdwenen de meeste molens uit het landschap.

Le moulin à vent de Lombeek-Notre-Dame au carrefour du temps. Jadis symboles de prospérité à la campagne, les moulins à vent ont pratiquement disparu du paysage après la révolution industrielle.

The windmill at Onze-Lieve-Vrouw-Lombeek at a cross-roads in time. Mills like this symbolized the prosperity of the countryside. Most of them disappeared after the industrial revolution.

Die Windmühle von Onze-Lieve-Vrouw-Lombeek an einer Kreuzung der Zeiten. Getreidemühlen waren ein Symbol des Wohlstands des platten Landes. Nach der Industrierevolution verschwanden sie aus der Landschaft.

Dit is het grootste kasteel van België. De landscommanderij Alden Biezen werd in 1220 door de Teutoonse Ridderorde gesticht. Het huidige waterkasteel dateert uit de zestiende eeuw.

Ceci est le plus grand château de Belgique. La grande commanderie Alden Biezen fut fondée par l'ordre des chevaliers Teutoniques. Le château actuel entouré d'eau date du 16ième siècle.

This is the biggest castle in Belgium. The military outpost Alden Biezen was built by the Teutonic Knighthood in 1220. The currently existing water castle dates from the sixteenth century.

Dies ist das größte Schloß von Belgien. Die Landeskommandantur Alden Biezen wurde 1220 vom teutonischen Ritterorden gebaut. Das heutige Wasserschloß datiert aus dem 16. Jahrhundert.

De haven van Zeebrugge is uitgegroeid tot een polyvalent transportcentrum. Het is een van de grootste Europese roll-on/roll-off havens waar grote volumes nieuwe wagens en containers mondiaal worden verscheept. Maar Zeebrugge is ook een toonaangevende energiehaven, een distributie knooppunt en een belangrijke passagiershaven.

Le port de Zeebrugge est devenue un centre de transport d'importance.
C'est une des plus grand ports transroutiers d'Europe où des grandes quantités des nou velles voitures et des con tainers sont transportées par bateau.
De plus, Zeebrugge est un port d'im por tance d'énergie, un routier de distribution et un grand port de paquebots.

The port of Seabruges has become a multifunctional centre of conveyance. It is one of the largest European roll-on/ roll-off ports in which large quantities of new cars and containers are being shipped.
Moreover, the harbour of Seabruges is a leading distributer of energy, a junction of distribution and an important passenger port.

Der Hafen von Seebrügge hat sich zu einem multifunktionalen Transportzentrum entwickelt.
Er ist einer der größten europäischen roll-on/roll-off Häfen (Umschlaghäfen), von dem große Stückzahlen von Neuwagen und Containern in alle Welt verschifft werden.
Aber Seebrügge ist auch einführender Energiehafen, ein Logistikzentrum und ein bedeutender Passagierhafen.

De meeste Belgen kennen dit merkwaardige gebouw. Vlakbij het strand in Oost-duinkerke staat dit bakstenen schip. Het is al meer dan een halve eeuw een hotel-restaurant.

La plupart des Belges connaissent ce bâtiment remarquable. Ce bateau de briques et de ciment s'est échoué tout près de la plage d'Oostdunkerke. Il y a plus d'un demi-siècle qu'il abrite un hôtel-restaurant.

Most Belgians will recognize this unusual building in the form of a brick ship near the beach in Oostduinkerke. It has been a hotel and a restaurant for over half a century.

Die meisten Belgier kennen es schon, dieses eigenartige Bauwerk in der Nähe des Strands von Oostduinkerke, aus Ziegelstein gemauert: ein Ozeanriese, seit über einem halben Jahrhundert Hotel und Restaurant.

In de Antwerpse haven
vecht een sproeiwagen tegen
opvliegend stof.

Dans le port d'Anvers une
voiture d'arrosage mène le
combat contre la poussière
qui s'envole.

In the Port of Antwerp
a watering cart is fighting
against raising dust.

Im Antwerpener Hafen
kämpft einen Sprühwagen
gegen den auffliegenden
Staub.

De oevers van de Leie in de omgeving van Kortrijk. Het vlas is een cultuurgewas dat nauw verbonden is met de tradities van het platteland. De vezels van de vlasstengels worden onder andere gebruikt voor de vervaardiging van touw en linnen.

Les rives de la Lys, dans les environs de Courtrai. La culture du lin est étroitement liée aux traditions paysannes. Les fibres du lin servent, entre autres, à fabriquer des cordes et de la toile.

The banks of the river Leie near Kortrijk. Flax is a crop that is closely bound up with rural traditions. The fibres of the flax-stalk are used to make rope and linen, among other things.

Die Ufer der Leie in der Nähe von Kortrijk. Der Flachsanbau ist eng mit den Traditionen des 'Flachen Landes' verbunden. Die Faser der Pflanze werden u.a. für die Herstellung von Seilen und Leinen verwendet.

De Belgische tuinbouw is een heel arbeidsintensieve sector die stilaan de gewone landbouw verdringt.

L'horticulture belge est un secteur à forte intensité de main-d'œuvre qui supplante progressivement l'agriculture normale.

Belgian horticulture is an extremely labour-intensive industry which is gradually ousting traditional farming.

Der Obst- und Gemüse-Anbau verdrängt in Belgien allmählich die traditionelle Landwirtschaft.

Meeuwen werden een paar jaar geleden alleen aan de kust gezien. Op zoek naar voedsel trekken ze nu steeds in grotere kolonies het binnen-land in. Ook in de winter is de kust een geliefde wandelplaats.

Il y a quelques années, les mouettes ne quittaient pas la côte. Elles partent maintenant en colonies toujours plus nombreuses en quête de nourriture dans l'arrière-pays. Même l'hiver, la côte est un lieu de promenade privilégié.

A few years ago, seagulls were only seen at the coast. Recently, however, they have been forming increasingly large colonies inland, in search of food. The coast is also a favourite place to walk in winter.

Bis vor wenigen Jahren wurden Möwen nur an der Küste gesichtet. Auf der Suche nach Nahrung ziehen sie aber jetzt in immer größeren Scharen ins Inland. Auch im Winter wird an der Küste viel gewandert.

Het strand in Blankenberge. De Belgische kust is slechts 64 kilometer lang, maar heeft een breed strand met fijn zand. Tijdens de zomermaanden is het een geliefkoosde vakantiebestemming voor Belgen en buitenlanders.

La plage à Blankenberge. Longue de 64 km seulement, la côte belge possède une large plage de sable fin. Pendant les mois d'été la côte est l'endroit de vacances préféré pour beaucoup de Belges ainsi que d'étrangers.

The beach at Blankenberge. Belgium only has 64 km of coast, but has a wide beach with fine sand. That makes it a favourite holiday destination for both Belgians and visitors every summer.

Der Strand von Blankenberge. Die belgische Küste ist nur 64 km. lang, hat aber breite Strände und feinen Sand. In den Sommermonaten ist sie ein beleibtes Urlaubsziel für Belgier wie Ausländer.

Het Torenhof in Kobbegem. Welvarende boeren bouwden het zo dat de muren en de torens van hun kasteelhoeve bescherming boden tegen rovers en andere gevaren.

Le Torenhof, à Kobbegem. Des fermiers prospères ont construit une ferme-château dont les murs et les tours les protégeaient contre les brigands et les autres dangers.

The Torenhof in Kobbegem. Wealthy farmers built fortified farms with walls and towers to protect themselves against thieves and other dangers.

Der 'Torenhof' in Kobbegem. Wohlhabende Bauern pflegten ihre Gutshöfe mit dicken Mauern und Türmen um sich gegen Rauber und andere Bedrohungen zu schützen.

Het Museum voor Midden-Afrika in Tervuren werd in 1908 gebouwd in opdracht van Koning Leopold II om belangstelling voor onze Afrikaanse kolonie te wekken.

Le Musée d'Afrique centrale, à Tervuren, a été construit en 1908 à la demande du roi Léopold II dans le but de susciter de l'intérêt pour la colonie royale.

The Central Africa Museum in Tervuren was built in 1908 at the order of King Leopold II to promote interest in our African colony.

Das Museum für Zentralafrika in Tervuren wurde 1908 im Auftrag des Könings Leopold II gebaut, der seine Untertanen für die Kolonien interessieren wollte.

De Duinenabdij in Koksijde dateert uit de twaalfde eeuw. Enkel de ruïnes blijven over als de stille getuigen van een groots verleden.

L'abbaye des Dunes à Coxyde date du 12ième siècle. Les ruines sont les seuls témoins silencieux d'un passé grandiose.

The dune abbey in Koksijde dates from the twelfth century. Only the ruins are the silent witnesses of a grand past.

Die Duinenabdij in Koksijde datiert aus dem 12. Jahrhundert. Nur die Ruinen sind die stillen Zeugen einer großen Vergangenheit.

In Ename ligt een van de mooiste archeologische sites van Vlaanderen. Het dorp was ooit een belangrijke haven aan de Schelde. Men ziet nog het grondplan en de resten van de abdij en de middeleeuwse haven.

A Ename se trouve un des plus beaux sites archéologiques de Flandre. A une époque le village fut un port important de l'Escaut. L'on voit encore le plan et les restes de l'abbaye et du port médiéval.

In Ename one of the most beautiful archaeological sites of Flanders is situated. Once this village was an important harbour along the Scheldt. One can still see the ground plan and the remains of the abbey and the medieval harbour.

In Ename liegt eine der schönsten archäologischen Grabungsstätten von Flandern. Das Dorf war irgendwann einmal der wichtigste Hafen an der Schelde. Man sieht noch den Grundriß und die Reste der Abtei und des mittel-alterlichen Hafens.

De petrochemie behoort tot de kernactiviteiten van de Antwerpse haven. In 1996 werden 6 miljoen ton ruwe aardolie en 9 miljoen ton aardoliederivaten aangevoerd.

La pétrochimie fait partie des activités principales du port d'Anvers. En 1996, 6 millions de tonnes de pétrole brut et 9 millions de dérivés du pétrole y ont été acheminés.

Petrochemistry is one of the core activities of the Port of Antwerp. Approximately 6 million tons of crude oil and 9 million tons of oil derivatives were shipped here in 1996.

Die petrochemische Industrie ist eine der Schwerpunkte im Antwerpener Hafen. 1996 wurden 6 Mio. Tonnen Rohöl und 9 Mio. Tonnen Erdölderivate verarbeitet.

Een pas aangelegd bungalowpark in het ontspannings- en verblijfspark Centerparks, aan het Zilvermeer in Mol.

Un parc de bungalows très récemment aménagé dans le parc de loisirs et de résidence Centerparks situé au bord du Zilvermeer à Mol.

A newly constructed bungalow park in the entertainment and residence park Centerparks, at the Zilvermeer in Mol.

Ein kürzlich angelegter Bungalowpark im Erholungs- und Vergnügungspark Centerparks am Zilvermeer in Mol.

The New British Cemetry in Passendale is een van de vele soldatenkerkhoven uit de frontstreek van de Eerste Wereldoorlog (1914-1918): het West-Vlaamse heuvelland en de IJzervlakte. In België rusten in totaal 149.924 Britse soldaten, waaronder 47.542 'only known to God', op 640 kerkhoven.

Le New British Cemetry de Passendale est l'un des nombreux cimetières militaires du front de la Première Guerre Mondiale (1914-1918): les collines flandriennes et la plaine de l'Yser. Un total de 149.924 soldats britanniques reposent sur le sol belge, dans 640 cimetières. 47.542 d'entre eux sont 'only known to God'.

The New British Cemetry in Passendale is one of the many military graveyards around the former battlegrounds of the First World War (1914-1918) - the hills of West Flanders and the plain around the river IJzer. A total of 149,924 Britisch soldiers are buried at 640 cemeteries in Belgium. Of these, 47,542 are 'only known to God'.

The New British Cemetry in Passendale ist einer der zahlreichen Soldatenfriedhöfe aus dem Ersten Weltkrieg (1914-1918). Die Front verlief durch das westflämische Hügelland und die IJzer-Ebene. Auf 640 belgischen Friedhöfen liegen insgesamt 149.924 britische Soldaten.

Een statige boerderij in het Waals-Brabantse Thorembais, met de typische gesloten bouwstructuur.

A stately farmhouse in Thorembais, Walloon Brabant, with the characteristic enclosed building style.

Une ferme majestueuse à Thorembais, dans le Brabant wallon, avec sa structure typique en carré fermé.

Ein stolzer Bauernhof in Thorembais, Wallonisch-Brabant, mit der typischen in sich geschloßenen Baustruktur.

De graaf van Liedekerke restaureerde het kasteel van Leefdaal aan het einde van de vorige eeuw. In 1626 werd dat kasteel gebouwd op de grondvesten van het eerste kasteel dat dateert uit de dertiende eeuw.

The count of Liedekerke restored Leefdaal Château towards the end of the nineteenth century. It was built in 1626 on the foundations of the original building, which dated back to the thirteenth century.

Le comte de Liedekerke a restauré le château de Leefdaal à la fin du siècle dernier. Ce château a été érigé en 1626 sur les fondations d'un premier château datant du début du treizième siècle.

Der Graf von Liedekerke restaurierte am Ende des vorigen Jahrhunderts Schloß Leefdaal. Es wurde 1626 auf den Fundamenten eines ersten Schlosses aus dem 13. Jh. erbaut.

Antwerpen is de tweede grootste haven van Europa met een maritieme trafiek van 110 miljoen ton per jaar en een toegevoegde handelswaarde van 233,7 miljard BEF. Antwerpen verzorgt op een heel uitgeruste en gespecialiseerde manier de algemene cargo: vooral de overslag van ijzer, staal, fruit, hout en auto's.

Anvers est le deuxième port en Europe, avec un trafic maritime de 110 millions de tonnes par an et une valeur commerciale ajoutée de 233,7 milliards BEF. Anvers assure de manière très outillée et très spécialisée le fret général: principalement le transbordement de fer, d'acier, de fruits, de bois et de voitures.

Antwerp is the second biggest port in Europe. It handles 110 million tons of cargo a year and generates a turnover of 233.7 miljard BEF. Antwerp's highly mechanized: special facilities handle general cargo of especially iron, steel, fruit, wood and transhipment of cars.

Antwerpen der zweitgrößte Hafen Europas: jährlich 110 Mio. Tonnen Frachtvolumen, 233,7 Mrd. BEF Warenwert. Im Hafen von Antwerpen wird Massengut aller Art, vor allem Eisen, Stahl, Obst, Holz und Automobile umgesetzt.

Een koolzaadveld in Schaffen, in de buurt van Diest. Koolzaad is doorgaans veevoeder maar wordt ook gebruikt voor de aanmaak van bio-diesel.

Un champs de colza à Schaffen, dans les environs de Diest. Le colza est habituelle-ment du fourrage, mais il est également utilisé pour la production d'un carburant biologique destiné aux moteurs diesel.

A field of rape in Schaffen, near Diest. Rape or colza is normally used as fodder, but is also used for the production of bio-diesel.

Ein Rapsfeld in Schaffen, in der Umgebung von Diest. Raps ist in der Regel Viehfutter, wird aber auch für die Herstellung von Biodiesel benutzt.

Groenten werden eerst gekweekt in de tuinen van kloosters en kastelen. Toen aan het einde van de vijftiende eeuw ook de rijke stadsbewoners groenten op hun bord wilden, begon men ze op grote schaal te telen.

Les légumes ont d'abord été cultivés dans les jardins des monastères et des châteaux. Il a fallu attendre la fin du 15ième siècle pour que les citadins riches en veuillent, eux aussi, sur leur table et pour que débute le maraîchage à grande échelle.

Vegetables were first cultivated in the gardens of monasteries and castles. It was only when wealthy townspeople also began to demand vegetables for their meals towards the end of the fifteenth century that cultivation began on a large scale.

Gemüse wurde ursprünglich nur in den Kleingärten der Schlösser und Abteien gezüchtet. Erst als am Ende des 15. Jh. auch die reichen Bürger der Städte Gemüse auf ihren Tellern haben wollten, wurde es großflächig angebaut.

Een Brabantse kasteelhoeve in Zoutleeuw, in Vochtig-Haspengouw. Dit is een hoeve van het gesloten type, afgeleid van het Frankische U-vormige hoevetype (stallen, woonhuis, schuur).

Une ferme-château brabançonne à Zoutleeuw, en Hesbaye-Humide. C'est une ferme du type clos, dérivée du type franc en forme de U (des étables, une maison d'habitation, une grange).

A Brabantine castle farm in Zoutleeuw, in Humid-Haspengouw. This is a farm of the closed type, derived from the Frankish farm type with the U-form (stables, dwelling house, barn).

Ein Brabanter Schloßhof in Zoutleeuw in Vochtig-Haspengouw. Dies ist ein Hof des geschlossenen Typs, abgeleitet aus dem fränkischen Hoftyp in U-Form (Ställe, Wohnhaus, Scheune).

Het strand van Knokke-Heist in de buurt van het natuurreservaat het Zwin. Bij laagwater worden op de vloedlijn kunstmatige meertjes gevormd waarin zich grondels, pitvissen en zwemkrabbetjes ophouden.

La plage de Knokke-Heist dans les environs de la réserve naturelle du Zwin. A marée basse de petits lacs artificiels dans lesquels s'attardent des gobies, des draconcules et des étrilles se forment le long du tracé qui indique la limite de la marée haute.

The beach of Knokke-Heist near the nature reserve Het Zwin. At low tide on the high-water mark small artificial lakes are formed which are occupied by gobies, dragonets and small sea crabs.

Der Strand von Knokke-Heist in der Nähe des Naturreservats Het Zwin. Bei Niedrigwasser werden an der Strandlinie künstliche Seen gebildet, in denen sich Gründlinge, Leierfische und Schwimmkrabben aufhalten.

Een van de weinige plaatsen in Vlaanderen waar de Schelde nog niet rechtgetrokken is. De stroom passeert over een breedte van 225 meter langs het dorp Sint-Amands.

Un des endroits peu nombreux de Flandre où l'Escaut n'a pas encore été 'rectifié'. Le fleuve passe sur une largeur de 225 mètres le long du village de Saint-Amand.

One of the few places in Flanders where the Scheldt has not yet been straightened. The river passes along the village Sint-Amands over a span of 225 meters.

Einer der wenigen Orte in Flandern, wo die Schelde noch nicht begradigt wurde. Der Strom passiert in einer Breite von 225 Meter das Dorf Sint-Amands.

Sneeuwlandschappen met bomen. Ze zijn in de Vlaamse schilderkunst meer dan eens vereeuwigd, onder andere door Pieter Bruegel, Valerius de Saedeleer en Constant Permeke.

Paysages enneigés avec arbres. Ils ont été célébrés depuis des siécles dans la peinture flamande, entre autres par Pieter Bruegel, Valerius de Saedeleer et Constant Permeke.

Snowy landscape with trees. Sights like this have been immortalised more than once in Flemish art by the likes of Pieter Brueghel, Valerius de Saedeleer and Constant Permeke.

Shneelandschaft mit Bäumen - ein beliebtes Motiv in der flämischen Malerei, u.a. für Pieter Bruegel, Valerius de Saedeleer und Constant Permeke.

Fruitbomen worden in hagen gesnoeid en laag bij de grond gehouden om het oogsten te vergemakkelijken. Dat kan de fruitkweker wel nadeel berokkenen bij vroege of late vorst.

Les arbres fruitiers sont taillés en haies de basse tige afin de rendre la ceuillette plus aisée. Mais cette taille peut causer des pertes à l'horticulteur en cas de gelée précoce ou tardive.

Fruit trees are pruned into hedges and kept near the ground to make harvesting easier. Unfortunately this also makes the fruit more vulnerable to early or late frosts.

Obstbäume werden wie Hecken und möglichst bodennah gestutzt. Bei Früh oder Spätfrost kann der Bauer dabei allerdings das Nachsehen haben.

De ruïne van een berg- of beltmolen, gebouwd op een kunstmatige heuvel om de aanvoer van het graan met paard en kar te vergemakkelijken. In België zijn er nog slechts 150 molens, 150 jaar geleden waren het er nog een kleine 3.000.

La ruine d'une colline et/ou d'un moulin sans rampe, construit sur une hauteur artificielle pour faciliter l'apport du blé sur une charrette tirée par un cheval. En Belgique il n'y a plus que 150 moulins; il y a 150 ans on en comptait encore presque 3.000.

The ruin of a windmill, built on an artificial hill in order to facilitate the supply of grain by means of horses and carts. In Belgium only 150 mills are left: 150 years ago there were still nearly 3.000 of them.

Die Ruine einer Hügel- oder Bergholländermühle, auf einem künstlichen Hügel gebaut, um die Anfuhr des Korns mit Pferd und Wagen zu vereinfachen. In Belgien gibt es nur noch 150 Mühlen, vor 150 Jahren waren es noch knapp 3.000.

Het slot van Marnix van Sint-Aldegonde in Bornem wordt nog altijd bewoond door die oude adellijke familie. Het is gelegen in de betoverende omgeving van de oude Schelde, waar de natuur nagenoeg ongeschonden is.

Le château de Marnix de Sainte-Aldegonde, à Bornem, est toujours habité par cette vieille famille noble. Il est situé dans le cadre enchanteur du bas Escaut où la nature est restée pratiquement intacte.

Marnix van Sint Aldegonde's castle at Bornem is still home to the same old, aristocratic family. It stands in the bewitching surroundings of the old Scheldt, with its virtually unspoiled nature.

Das Schloß des Marnix von Sankt Aldegonde in Bornem wird immer noch von einer adligen Familie bewohnt. Es liegt in der bezaubernden, nahezu unberührten Umgebung der alten Schelde.

48

Het middeleeuwse
stadscentrum van Gent met
de Sint-Baafskathedraal en het
belfort. Op de voorgrond het
Gravensteen in romaanse stijl.

Le centre médiéval de la ville
de Gand avec la cathédrale
Saint-Bavon, le Beffroi et à
l'avant-plan le château des
Comtes en style romane.

The medieval city centre of
Ghent with the Sint-Baafs
Cathedral and the Belfry.
On the foreground the
Gravensteen castle in
Romanesque style.

Das mittelalterliche Stadt-
zentrum von Gent mit der
Sint-Baafskathedrale und dem
Belfort und im Vordergrund
der Gravensteen im
romanischen Stil.

Het centrum van Mechelen met de imposante Sint-Romboutskathedraal in Brabantse hoog-gotiek. De veertiende-eeuwse lakenhalle en het laat-gotische paleis van de Grote Raad herbergen het stadhuis aan de overkant van de markt.

Le centre de Malines avec l'imposante cathédrale Saint-Rombaut en premier gothique brabançon. La Halle aux draps et le palais du Grand Conseil en gothique tardif hébergent l'hôtel de ville, de l'autre côté du marché.

The centre of Mechelen with the impressive Sint-Rombouts Cathedral in a Brabantine High-Gothic style. The fourteenth century Lakenhal and its Late-Gothic palace of the Great Council contain the city hall across of the market place.

Das Zentrum von Mechelen mit der imposanten Sint-Romboutskathedrale in Brabanter Hochgotik. Die Tuchhalle aus dem 14. Jahrhundert und der spätgotische Palast des Groote Raad beherbergen das Rathaus an der gegenüberliegenden Seite des Marktes.

De dodengang in Diksmuide strekt zich over een lengte van twee kilometer langs de IJzer uit. Het zijn de overblijfselen van de loopgraven uit de Eerste Wereldoorlog toen hier het eindoffensief tegen de Duitse bezetter werd beslecht.

L'allée des morts à Dixmude s'étend sur un longueur de deux kilomètres le long de l'Yser. Ce sont les restants des tranchées de la Première Guerre mondiale lorsque en ce lieu l'offensive finale contre l'occupant allemand fut entamée avec succès.

The passage of death in Diksmuide extends over a length of two kilometres along the river the IJzer. These are the remains of the trenches from the first World War when a final offensive against the German occupying forces was settled.

Der Dodengang in Diksmuide erstreckt sich über eine Länge von zwei Kilometer entlang der Ijzer. Dies sind die Überreste des Schützen- grabens aus dem Ersten Weltkrieg, als hier die Endoffensive gegen die deutschen Besatzer abgeschlossen wurde.

Het Napoleonfort in Oostende volledig in de stijl van Vauban: een perfecte pentagoon met water- omwalling. Oostende was voor Napoleon de ideale uitvalshaven voor de aanval op Engeland.

Le fort Napoléon à Ostende entièrement dans le style de Vauban : un pentagone parfait et des remparts entourés d'eau. Ostende était pour Napoléon le port de départ idéal pour prendre l'Angleterre d'assaut.

The Napoleon Fortress in Ostend was completely built in the style of Vauban: a perfectly constructed pentagon and a waterwall. For Napoleon Ostend was a strategic place during the attack on England.

Das Napoleonfort in Ostende, vollständig im Stil von Vauban: ein perfektes Pentagon mit Wasserumwallung. Ostende war für Napoleon der perfekte Ausfallhafen für den Angriff auf England.

De 'stad' Damme telt slechts 800 inwoners. In de vroege Middeleeuwen had Brugge via Damme toegang tot de zee. Op het einde van de dertiende eeuw begon de haven van Damme te verzanden.

La 'ville' de Damme ne compte que 800 habitants. Au début du Moyen-Age, la ville de Bruges avait accès à la mer par Damme. Le port de Damme a commencé à s'ensabler à la fin du treizième siècle.

The 'city' of Damme only has 800 inhabitants. In the early Middle Ages, Damme provided Bruges with its access to the sea. The port at Damme began to silt up towards the end of the thirteenth century.

Die 'Stadt' Damme zählt nur 800 Einwohner. In frühen Mittelalter hatte Brügge über Damme einen direkten Zugang zum Meer. Am Ende des 13. Jh. fing der Hafen von Damme an zu versanden.

Alvorens in Leuven aan te komen, trekt de Dijle een spoor van meanders door de velden en de bossen van Heverlee.

Before entering Leuven the river Dijle leaves a track of meanders through the fields and the woods of Heverlee.

Avant d'atteindre Louvain la Dyle forme des méandres à travers les champs et les forêts de Heverlee.

Die Dijle zieht ihre mäanderartige Spur durch die Felder und die Wälder von Heverlee, bevor sie in Löwen ankommt.

Doornik met de Notre-Dame-kathedraal, het meesterwerk van de romaanse bouwkunst uit de Scheldestreek. Doornik is na Tongeren de oudste stad van België. Ze bezit het oudste belfort (vroeg-gotisch) van het land, een renaissance-lakenhalle en meer dan een dozijn oude kerken.

Tournai est la cathédrale Notre-Dame: le chef-d'oeuvre de l'architecture romane de la région de l'Escaut.
Plus ancienne ville de Belgique après Tongres. Tournai possède le plus vieux beffroi (gothique précoce) du pays, une halle aux draps de la Renaissance et plus d'une douzaine d'églises anciennes.

Tournai with Notre Dame Cathedral, the masterpiece of Romanesque architecture in the Scheldt region. Tournai is the second eldest city in Belgium (after Tongeren). It has the eldest belfry (Early Gothic) in the country, a Renaissance Cloth Hall and more than a dozen old churches.

Tournai mit der Liebfrauen-kathedrale, dem Meisterwerk romanischer Baukunst im Scheldetal. Tounai ist, nach Tongeren, die zweitälteste Stadt Belgiens. Hier steht der älteste, frühgotische Bergfried des Landes, sowie eine Tuchhalle im Renaissancestil und über ein Dutzend alter Kirchen.

Het kasteel en het landgoed van de schilder Pieter Paul Rubens in Elewijt. In dit zomerverblijf bracht de barokke schilder zijn laatste levensjaren door.

Le château et la résidence de campagne du peintre Pierre Paul Rubens à Elewijt. Le peintre baroque vécut ses dernières années dans cette résidence d'été.

Painter Pieter Paul Rubens' castle and estate in Elewijt. In this summer home the baroque painter spent his last living years.

Das Schloß und das Landgut des Malers Pieter Paul Rubens in Elewijt. Auf diesem Sommersitz verbrachte der Maler des Barock seine letzten Lebensjahre.

De toegangsweg tot deze hoeve is volledig afgezoomd met Japanse kerselaars, een sierboom die ongebruikelijk is als borderboom in landbouwgebied.

The access road is completely surrounded with Japanese cherry trees. This is a kind of ornamental tree which is not commonly used as a border region tree in agricultural areas.

Le chemin d'accès vers cette ferme est entièrement bordé de cerisiers japonais, un arbre ornemental inhabituel comme arbre de bordure dans une zone agricole.

Die Zugangsstraße zu diesem Gehöft wird vollständig von japanischer Kirsche gesäumt, einem Zierbaum, der als Begrenzungsbaum im landwirtschaftlichen Bereich ungebräuchlich ist.

Een zeldzaam beeld van een natuurlijke scheiding met bomen tussen twee akkers. Doorgaans hebben de verkavelingen er voor gezorgd dat alle bomen verdwenen.

Une image rare d'une séparation naturelle faite d'arbres entre deux champs. En règle générale, les parcellements ont fait en sorte que tous les arbres ont disparu.

A rare image of a natural boundary of trees between two fields. Generally the parcelling has resulted in the disappearance of all trees.

Ein seltenes Bild einer natürlichen Grenze aus Bäumen zwischen zwei Ackerflächen. In der Regel haben die Parzellierungen dafür gesorgt, daß alle Bäume verschwanden.

Vergeten – of liever: ge-
spaard – midden in het veld:
een boom midden op een
plateau in de Ardennen.

Oublié ou plutôt épargné
en plein champs: un arbre
au centre d'un plateau dans
les Ardennes.

Forgotten or rather spared in
the middle of the field: a tree
in the middle of a plateau in
the Ardennes.

Vergessen oder besser
geschont mitten im Feld:
ein Baum mitten auf einem
Plateau in den Ardennen.

Indian Summer op de golfbaan van Tervuren. De golfsport heeft zich in België de jongste jaren fel ontwikkeld, ondanks de bezwaren van de milieubewegingen tegen de aanleg van golfterreinen. Vooral dankzij de democratisering van die sporttak, telt België momenteel een dertigtal volwaardige golfbanen.

Eté indien sur le golf de Tervuren. Le golf s'est fortement développé ces dernières années en Belgique, malgré l'opposition des mouvements écologistes à l'installation de terrains de golf. C'est principalement à la démocratisation de ce sport que la Belgique doit actuellement une trentaine de terrains de golf dignes de ce nom.

Indian Summer on the golf-course at Tervuren. Golf has been developing rapidly in Belgium in recent years, despite environmentalists' objections to the laying of courses. Belgium now has 30 fullyfledged golf clubs, mainly thanks to the democratization of the sport.

Indian Summer am Golfplatz von Tervuren. Der Sport hat sich in Belgien in den jüngsten Jahren, trotz des Protestes der Umweltschützer gegen neue Golfplätze, rasant entwickelt. Inzwischen ist Golf zum Volkssport geworden: Belgien hat heute nicht weniger als dreißich hochwertige Golfplätze.

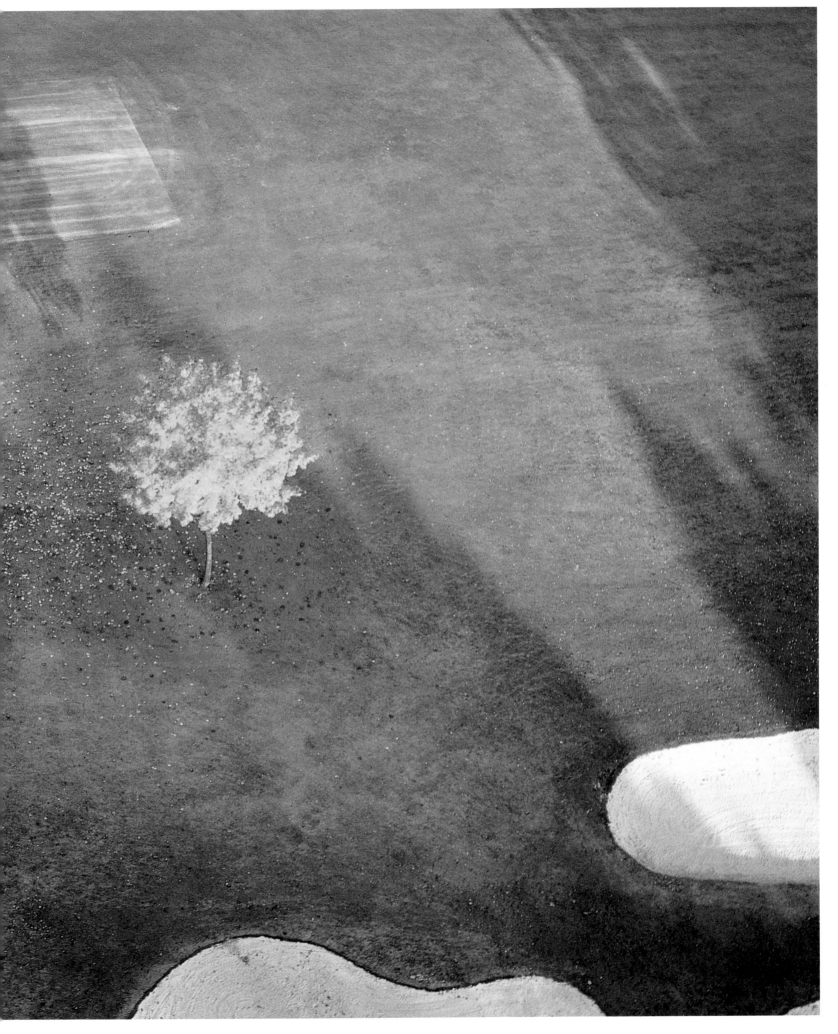

Le Grand Hornu in de buurt van Bergen is een voormalige industriële site. De fabrieksgebouwen waren voorzien van woongelegenheid. De site zou binnen afzienbare tijd ook het eerste museum voor hedendaagse kunst in Wallonië moeten herbergen.

Le Grand Hornu, dans la région montoise, est un ancien site industriel construit selon le système des bâtiments d'usine dotés de logements. Le site devrait également abriter, dans un proche avenir, le premier véritable musée d'art contemporain de Wallonie.

Le Grand Hornu, near Mons, is a former industrial site combining factory buildings with homes. There are plans to house Wallonia's first real museum of contemporary art here.

Le Grand Hornu in der Nähe von Mons, eine ehemalige Industrieanlage.
Dem Bergwerk angeschlossen ist eine Arbeitersiedlung.
Die Siedlung soll demnächst das erste Museum zeitgenössischer Kunst in Wallonien beherbergen

De Forges de Clabecq is een van de laatste grote staalgieterijen uit het zuiden van het land.

Les Forges de Clabecq sont une des dernières grandes usines sidérurgiques du sud du pays.

The Forges de Clabecq is one of the last large steel foundries in the south of the country.

Die Forges de Clabecq ist eine der letzten großen Stahlgießereien im Süden des Landes.

Cockerill-Sambre in Charleroi. Het Bekken van Charleroi leverde, toen dat steenkool- en industriegebied nog op volle toeren draaide, de helft van de totale Waalse steenkoolproductie.
Door de aanwezigheid van steenkool was een deel van de staalnijverheid er gevestigd.

Cockerill-Sambre à Charleroi. Le Bassin de Charleroi assurait, lorsque cette région houillère et industrielle tournait à plein régime, la moitié de la production wallonne de charbon.
La présence du charbon explique pourquoi une partie de l'industrie de l'acier s'y est installée.

Cockerill-Sambre in Charleroi. The Charleroi basin once accounted for half of all Wallonia's coal output, in the days when this industrial and mining region was still at its peak. The presence of coal attracted part of the country's steel industry to the area.

Die Industrieanlange 'Cockerill-Sambre' in Charleroi. Als das Revier noch auf vollen Touren lief, kam die Hälfte der gesamten wallonischen Kohle aus dem Becken von Charleroi.
Die Bergwerke zogen die Stahlindustrie an.

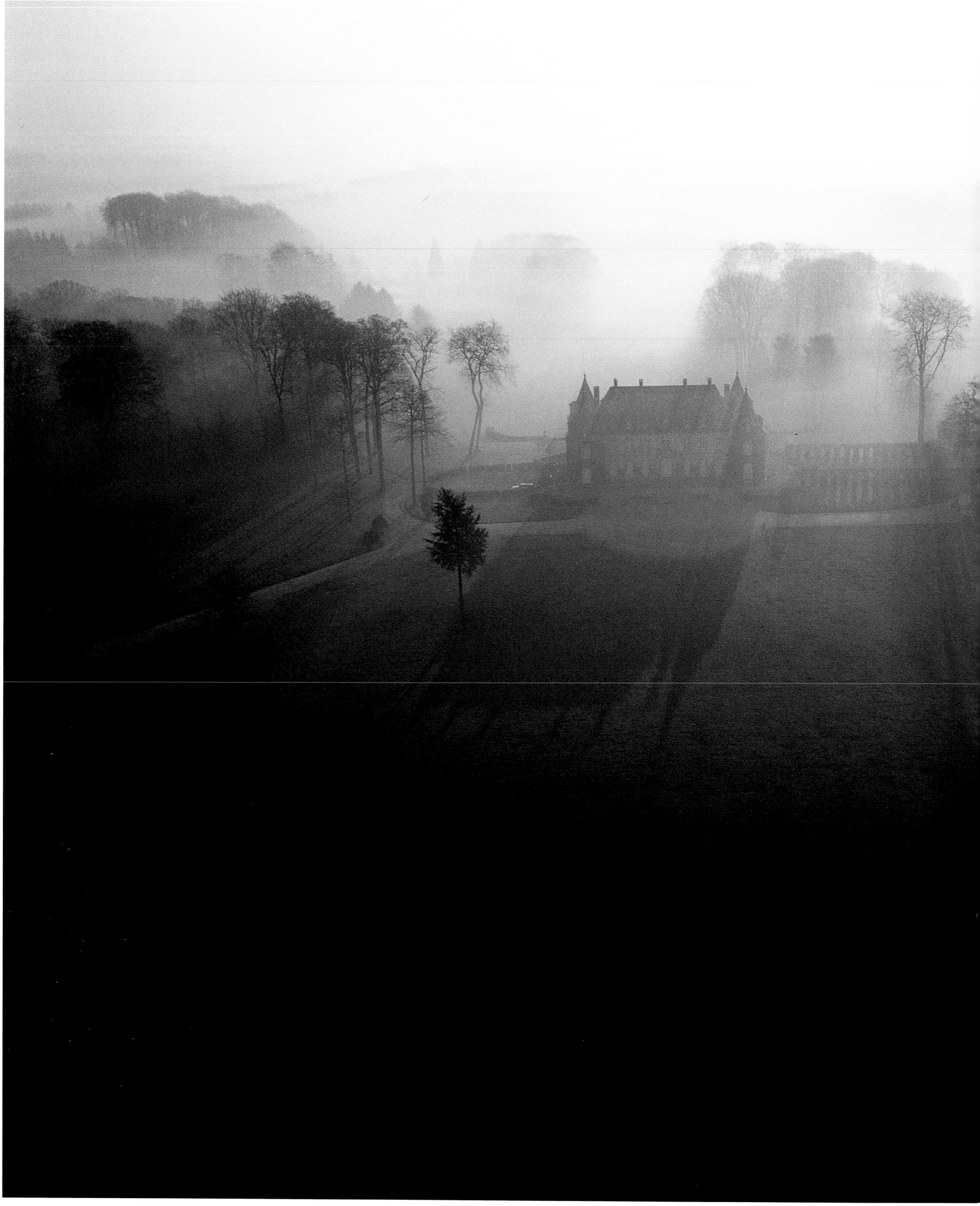

Het kasteel van Terhulpen wordt omringd door 220 hectaren gazon, paden, bossen en vijvers. Deze residentie van de familie Solvay behoort nu toe aan het Waalse Gewest. Het kasteel dateert uit de negentiende eeuw en is in feite een grandioze villa.

The château at La hulpe is surrounded by 220 hectares of lawn, paths, woods and lakes. The former mansion of the Solvay family now belongs to the Walloon Region. The château dates from the nineteenth century and is actually a magnificent villa.

Le château de La Hulpe est entouré de 220 hectares de gazon, de sentiers, de bois et d'étangs. Cette ancienne résidence de la famille Solvay appartient maintenant à la région Wallonne. Le château date du dix-neuvième siècle et est, en fait, une villa aux dimensions grandioses.

Das Schloß von Terhulpen mit seinen 220 Hektar Rasen, Pfaden, Wäldern und Teichen. Die einstige Residenz der Familie Solvay ist heute im Besitz der Wallonischen Regionalverwaltung. Das Schloß aus dem vorigen Jahrhundert ist in Wirklichkeit eine grandiose Villa.

De abdijruïne van Aulne in Henegouwen. In de twaalfde eeuw was dit een florissante abdij. Volgens de legende werd zij in de zevende eeuw gesticht door de heilige Landelin. De sansculotten vernietigden het gebouw in 1794. De kostbare bibliotheek ging in de vlammen op.

Les ruines de l'abbaye d'Aulne, dans le Hainaut. L'abbaye a connu sa période de prospérité au douzième siècle. D'après la légende, elle a été fondée au septième siècle par Saint Audelin. Les sans-culottes rasèrent entièrement le bâtiment en 1794 et firent partir en fumée une bibliothèque d'une grande valeur.

The ruined abbey at Aulne in Hainaut. The institution flourished in the twelfth century. According to the legend, it was founded by Saint Landelinus. The building was destroyed by French revolutionaries in 1794, who also burned down the priceless library.

Die Abteiruine von Aulne im Hennegau. Im 12.Jh. war sie eine blühende Abtei, laut Legende im 7.Jh. vom Heiligen Landelin gegründet. Die Sansculotten zerstörten 1794 das Gebäde und brannten die kostbare Bibliothek ab.

De abdij van Maredsous is vooral beroemd voor haar kazen en stevig abdijbier. Dit benedictijnerklooster ontstond in 1872 en groeide uit tot een cultuurcentrum met belangrijke geleerden.

L'abbaye de Maredsous est surtout appréciée pour ses fromages et sa forte bière d'abbaye. Fondé en 1872, seulement, ce monastère obéissant à la règle de Saint-Benoît est un centre culturel où de grands érudits poursuivent leurs recherches.

The abbey at Maredsous is famous for its cheeses and strong abbey beer. The Benedictine monastery was founded in 1872 and became a cultural centre with leading scholars.

Die Abtei von Maredsous, bekannt für ihren Käse und ihr Starkbier. Das Benediktiner-kloster entstand 1872 und wurde bald zu einem Kultur- und Forschungszentrum.

De abdij van Villers-la-Ville is ongetwijfeld de meest indrukwekkende ruïne van België. De geschiedenis van die abdij gaat terug tot 1146. Samen met Cluny groeide het klooster uit tot een van de belangrijkste religieuze centra van West-Europa.

The abbey at Villers-la Ville is undoubtedly Belgium's most impressive ruin. The history of this monastery goes back to 1146. Together with Cluny, it once was one of the most important religious centres in western Europe.

L'abbaye de Villers-la-Ville est la ruine la plus impression-nante de Belgique. Avec Cluny, ce monastère, dont la création remonte à 1146, était l'un des centres réligieux les plus importants d'Europe occidentale.

Die Abtei von Villers-la-Ville ist zweifelsohne die eindrucksvollste Ruine Belgiens. Ihre Geschichte geht bis ins Jahr 1146 zurück. Das Kloster war im Mittelalter, neben Cluny, eines der wichtigsten religiösen Zentren Europas.

Luik ligt op de samenvloeiiing van de Maas en de Ourthe. De Maas verdeelt de stad in twee delen die door zestien bruggen met elkaar verbonden worden. Het stadscentrum wordt gedomineerd door de steile citadel.

Liège se trouve au confluent de la Meuse et de l'Ourthe. La Meuse divise la ville en deux parties reliées par seize ponts. Le centre de la ville est dominé par une citadelle abrupte.

The rivers Meuse and Ourthe flow together in Liège. The Meuse divides the city in two and is crossed by 16 bridges. The city centre is dominated by steep slopes leading to the citadel.

Lüttich liegt am Zusammenfluß von Maas und Ourthe. Die Maas teilt die Stadt in zwei Hälften, die von 16 Brücken miteinander verbunden werden. Die Innenstadt wird von der Zitadelle überragt.

Dinant is een parel aan de oever van de Maas. Deze sfeervolle stad is een van de belangrijkste toeristische trekpleisters van het land. Adolphe Sax, de uitvinder van de saxofoon, werd hier geboren.

Dinant est une perle déposée en bord de Meuse. Cette charmante petite ville est l'une des principales attractions touristiques du pays. C'est ici qu'est né Adolphe Sax, l'inventeur du saxophone.

Dinant is a jewel on the banks of the Meuse.
This atmospheric city is one of the country's most important tourist attractions. Adolphe Sax, inventor of the saxophone, was born here.

Dinant - ein Perle am Ufer der Maas. Die gemütliche Stadt ist eines der wichtigsten touristischen Ziele des Landes. Adolphe Sax, der Vater des Saxophons, wurde hier geboren.

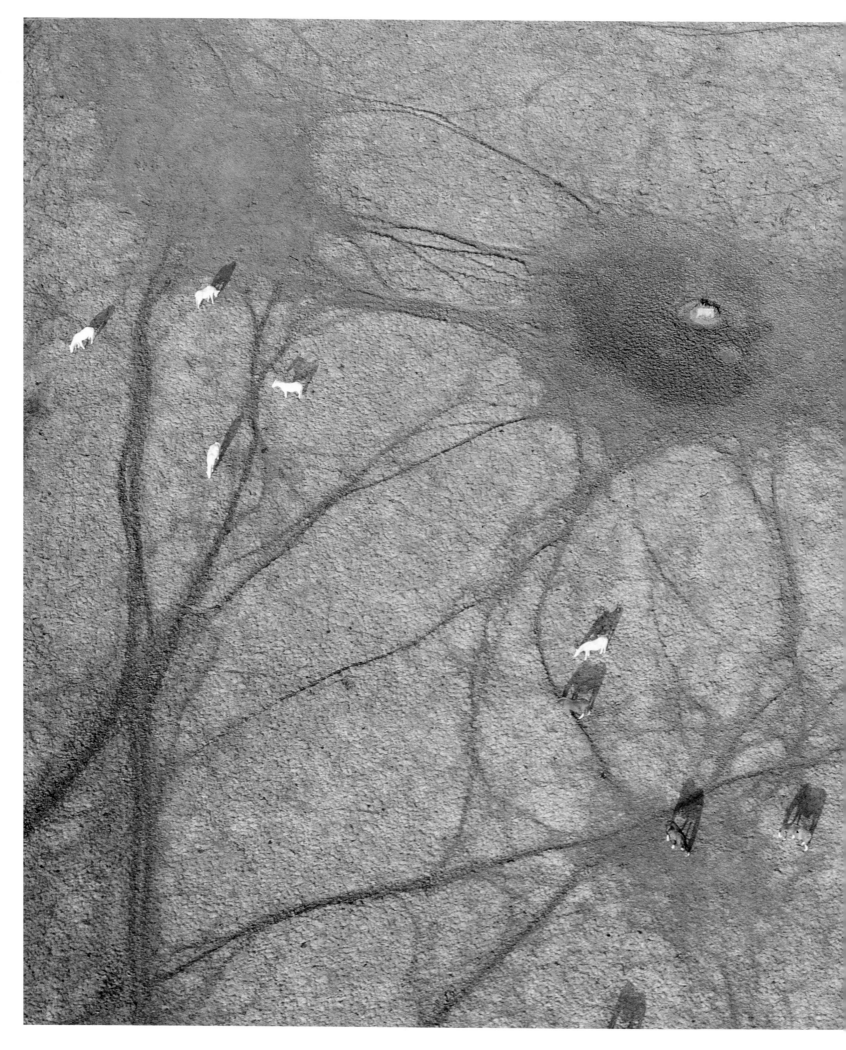

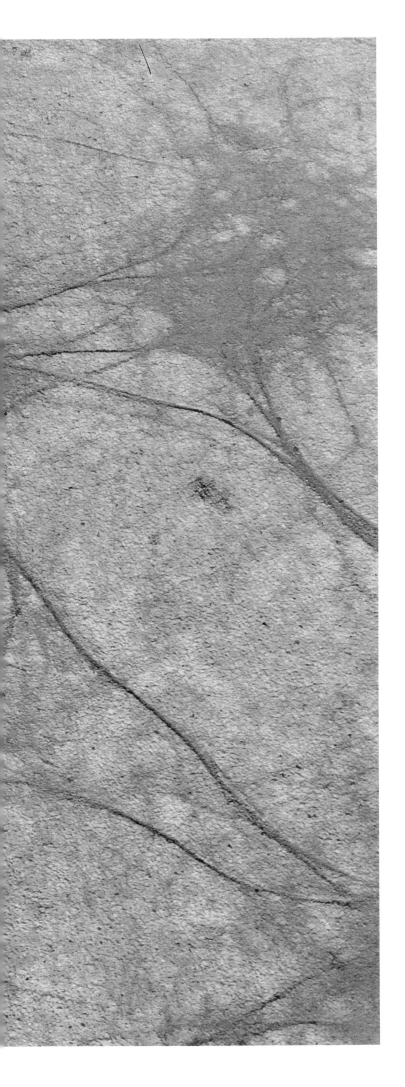

Hoog boven in de lucht blijft
het landschap een onuit-
puttelijke bron van inspiratie.
Deze drinkplaats voor paarden
lijkt wel een zenuwcel.

Viewed from high in the sky,
the landscape remains an
inexhaustible source of
inspiration. This watering
place for horses resembles
the layout of a neuron.

Vu du ciel, le paysage est
une source intarissable
d'inspiration. Cet abreuvoir à
chevaux ne ressemble-t-il pas
à une cellule nerveuse?

Da oben in der Luft ist die
Landschaft immer wieder eine
unerschöpfliche Inspirations-
quelle. Diese Pferdetränke
z. B.: sie ähnelt einer
Nervenzelle.

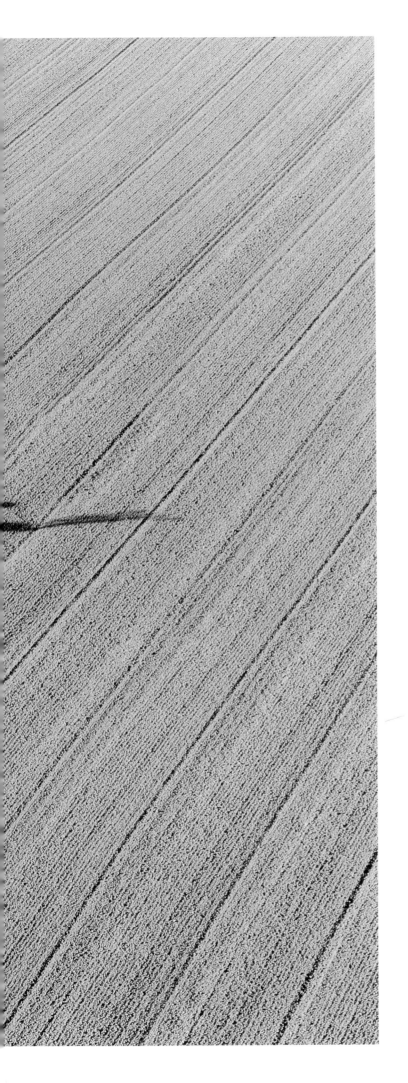

Een relaishuisje van de elektriciteitsmaatschappij midden in de velden. Er liep zo goed als zeker een smal weggetje naartoe maar dat wordt steevast door de boeren omgeploegd.

A relay post of an electricity company amidst the fields. In all probability a small road must have led to it, but it has been ploughed away by the farmers.

Une maisonnette servant de relais à la compagnie d'électricité en plein champs. Un sentier étroit y conduisit très probablement. De tels chemins sont invariablement labourés par les agriculteurs.

Ein Relaishäuschen der Elektrizitätsgesellschaft mitten auf den Feldern, ziemlich sicher führte dort einmal ein schmaler Weg hin, aber der wurde immer wieder von den Bauern umgepflügt.

Ingepakte hooistapels in het zuiden van België. In België zijn er nog tal van open agrarische landschappen: het land van Herve, Haspengouw, Zuid-Brabant en de Henegouwse leemstreek zorgen voor dit soort malse graslandschappen die hoofdzakelijk een leem-ondergrond hebben.

Haystacks in southern Belgium. The country still has many open farming landscapes. The regions of Herve, Haspengauw, southern Brabant and Hainaut all feature this kind of soft, grassy landscape, mostly on clay soil.

Ballots de foin emballés dans le sud de la Belgique. La Belgique compte encore un grand nombre de paysages agricoles ouverts: le pays de Herve, la Hesbaye, le Brabant wallon et la région argileuse du Hainaut produisent ce genre de paysages herbagers rassurants, au sous-sol principalement argileux.

Eingepackte Heubündel im Süden. Noch hat Belgien weite, agrarische Landschaften: im Herveland, Haspengau, Südbrabant und Hennegau verdanken wir dem häufig lehmigen Boden saftige, grüne Wiesen.

Een luchtballon boven Waals-Brabant. In 1783 lieten de gebroeders Montgolfier een eerste luchtballon van linnen en papier op. Het zou nog langer dan een eeuw duren vooraleer een vliegtuig zou opstijgen.

Un ballon survole le Brabant wallon. C'est en 1783 que les frères Montgolfier ont fait voler leur premier ballon de toile et de papier. Il a fallu attendre plus d'un siècle pour qu'un avion en fasse autant.

A hot-air balloon over Walloon Brabant. The Montgolfier brothers launched the first linen and paper balloon in 1783 almost a century before the first aeroplane took off.

Ein Luftballon über dem wallonischen Teil Brabants. 1783 starteten die Brüder Montgolfier den ersten Luftballon aus Leinen und Papier. Bis zum Start eines Flugzeuges sollte es noch über ein Jahrhundert dauern.

De Leeuw van Waterloo bewaakt de nagedachtenis van de 45.000 soldaten die in 1815 sneuvelden bij de slag van Waterloo.

Le Lion de Waterloo veille sur la mémoire des 45.000 soldats tombés en 1815 à la bataille de Waterloo.

The Lion of Waterloo watches over the monument dedicated to the 45,000 soldiers who died in the battle here in 1815.

Der 'Löwe von Waterloo' wacht über die 45.000 Soldaten, die hier 1815 in der Schlacht fielen.

Op het Canal du Centre functioneren nog altijd drie hydraulische liften die al honderd jaar in bedrijf zijn. De liften moeten de schepen toelaten een niveauverschil van 4 tot 17 meter te overbruggen en werken volkomen op waterenergie.

Sur le Canal du Centre, on peut encore voir fonctionner trois ascenseurs hydrauliques mis en service depuis un siècle. Les ascenseurs font franchir aux bateaux une dénivellation de 4 à 17 mètres. Ils fonctionnent entièrement à l'énergie hydraulique.

Three hydraulic elevators, which have been in operation for a hundred years, still raise and lower traffic on the Canal du Centre. They were designed to convey barges over a difference in height between 4 and 17 metres, working entirely by means of waterenergy.

Auf dem 'Canal du Centre' funktionieren immer noch drei Schiffsaufzüge, die bereits seit hundert Jahren in Betrieb sind. Mit Hilfe dieser Aufzüge können die Schiffe Niveauunterschiede von 4 bis 17m. überwinden. Die aufzüge werden ausschliesslich mit Wasserkraft betrieben.

Een verbindingsweg die nooit is afgemaakt en dus eindigt op een rotonde.

Une voie de communication qui n'a jamais été achevée et qui par conséquent prend tout simplement fin à une rotonde.

A connecting road which has never been finished and which just ends with a roundabout.

Eine Verbindungsweg, der niemals fertiggestellt wurde und deshalb in einem Kreisverkehr endet.

In de Ardennen zijn de meeste bossen bestemd voor opbrengsthout, de poëzie van de Ardense wouden moet al eens wijken voor de kap.

In the Ardennes most woods are used for the production of timber; sometimes even this sheer poetry must disappear for chopping.

La plupart des forêts dans les Ardennes sont destinées à rapporter du bois. Parfois la poésie des forêts ardennaises doit céder le pas à l'abattage des arbres.

In den Ardennen dienen die meisten Wälder der Nutzholzgewinnung, die Poesie der Ardennenwälder mußte schon manchmal dem Holzeinschlag weichen.

84

La Collégiale in Nijvel: de kerk werd vernield in mei 1940 toen de stad na een bombardement in de vlammen opging. Herrezen uit zijn as, mooier dan ooit.

La Collégiale à Nivelles : l'église fut détruite en mai 1940 lors de l'incendie de la ville après un bombardement. Relevée de ses cendres, plus belle que jamais.

The Collegiale in Nivelles: the church was destroyed in May 1940 when, after a bombardment, the city went up in flames. Risen out of the ashes, with a unique and matchless beauty.

La Collègiale in Nivelles: die Kirche wurde im Mai 1940 vernichtet, als die Stadt nach einem Bombardement in Flammen aufging. Wiedererstanden aus ihrer Asche, ist sie schöner, als je zuvor.

De geschiedenis van het elegante kasteel van Vêves gaat terug tot het jaar 600. Het romantische bouwwerk met zes torens werd opgetrokken op een rots in een dal.

L'histoire de l'élégant château de Vêves remonte à l'an 600. Cette construction romantique à six tours a été érigée sur un rocher au creux d'une vallée.

The history of the elegant château at Vêves goes back to the year 600. The romantic building with its six towers was built on a rocky outcrop in a valley.

Die Geschichte des eleganten Schloßes Vêves reicht bis ins Jahr 600. Das romantisch anmutende Bauwerk mit seinen sechs Türmen steht auf einem Felsen im Tal.

Een graancirkel in Durbuy.
Deze graancirkel is met
zekerheid niet door buiten-
aardse wezens gemaakt maar
door aardbewoners. Helemaal
in het midden van de cirkel
staat een tafel met fris
Belgisch bier.

A crop circle in Durbuy.
This crop circle is certainly not
the work of extraterrestrials,
but of earthlings. The table in
the middle of the circle with
fresh Belgian beer on it seems
to be proof enough.

Un champ de blé en forme
d'un labyrinthe. Cet labyrinthe
n'est certainement pas fait par
des extraterrestres. Ce sont
des êtres humains qui ont
formé ce jardin d'agrément.
Une table avec de la bierre
Belge, bien fraiche, se trouve
au milieu du circle.

Ein Getreidekreis in Durbuy.
Diesen Getreidekreis haben
mit Sicherheit nicht
außerirdische Wesen
gemacht, sondern
Erdbewohner. Ganz in der
Mitte des Kreises steht ein
Tisch mit kühlem Belgischem
Bier.

Een plateau in de Hoge Venen. De begroeiing is vergelijkbaar met die van de heide. Dit is beschermd natuurgebied met zeldzame fauna en flora.

A plateau in the Hautes Fagnes. The vegetation is comparable to the one of the heath land. This is a protected nature reserve with a rare fauna and flora.

Un plateau dans les Hautes Fagnes. La végétation est comparable à celle de la bruyère. Ceci est un zone naturelle protégée, dans laquelle il y a une végétation rare.

Eine Hochebene im Hohen Venn. Die Begrünung ist mit der Heide vergleichbar. Dies ist eine geschützte Natur-landschaft mit seltenem Bewuchs.

Een typisch voorbeeld van een cultuurbos in de lente. Het kaphout op de percelen wordt omzoomd met sierbomen.

A typical example of a culture wood in spring. The timber used for chopping on the parcels is surrounded with ornamental trees.

Un exemple typique d'une forêt de rendement au printemps. Dans les parcelles le bois coupé est liséré d'arbres ornementaux.

Ein typisches Beispiel für einen Kulturwald im Frühling. Das eingeschlagene Holz auf den Parzellen wird mit einem Streifen aus Zierbäumen begrenzt.

Het kasteel van Jehay-
Bodegnée werd tussen de
zestiende en zeventiende
eeuw verbouwd op de grondvesten van een middeleeuwse
burcht. Dit prachtige jachtslot
valt op door zijn dambord-
façade, een bonte mengeling
van witte steen en zandsteen.

The château at Jehay-
Bodegnée was built in the
sixteenth and seventeenth
century on the foundations of
a medieval castle. This fine
hunting lodge stands out for
its chequered facade, made up
of a varied mixture of white
stone and sandstone.

Le château de Jehay-Bodegnée
a été reconstruit entre le
seizième et le dix-septième
siècles, sur les fondations
díune forteresse médiévale.
Ce magnifique pavillon de
chasse frappe par sa façade en
damier composée d'un
mélange hardi de pierre
blanche et de grés.

Das Schloß von Jehay-
Bodegnée wurde im 16./17. Jh.
auf den Fundamenten einer
mittelalterlichen Burg gebaut.
Das prunkvolle Jagdschloß
zeichnet sich durch seine
Schachbrettfassade aus
verschiedenen Steinarten aus.

Lokale amateurvoetbalclubs, elk dorp heeft er wel een. In België is voetbal synoniem voor een intens verenigings- leven.

Clubs de football amateurs et locaux, chaque village possède le sien. En Belgique, le football symbolise l'intensité de la vie associative.

Every village has its own amateur football club. Football is an important part of social life in Belgium.

Fußballklubs, Amateurvereine - jedes Dorf hat mindestens einen davon. In Belgien ist Fußball nichts anderes als heftige Vereinsmeierei...

Een idyllisch hoekje met koeien, haast een tafereel van de luministische schilder Emile Claus, in Sint-Brixius-Rode, op nauwelijks een paar kilometer van het centrum van Brussel.

Un coin idyllique avec des vaches, presque une scène de l'artiste luministe Emile Claus, à Sint-Brixius-Rode, à quelques kilomètres à peine du centre de Bruxelles.

An idyllic spot with cows it could almost be a scene from a painting by the Luminist artist Emile Claus. This is Sint-Brixius-Rode, a few kilometres from the centre of Brussels.

Die idyllische Ecke mit den Kühen mutet wie eine Szene des luministischen Malers Emile Claus an in Sint-Brixius-Rode, nur wenige Kilometer von der Brüsseler City entfernt.

Een typische sluis uit de negentiende eeuw op de rivier de Samme in Seneffe. De rivier wordt geflankeerd door een jaagpad waar de schepen tot na de Tweede Wereldoorlog gejaagd (getrokken) werden door paarden.

A typical sluice from the nineteenth century on the river Samme, in Seneffe. The river is flanked by a towing-path where the ships were pulled by horses until after the Second World War.

Une écluse typique du dix-neuvième siècle sur la rivière la Samme, à Seneffe. La rivière est bordée d'un chemin de halage d'où jusqu'après la deuxième guerre mondiale les bateaux étaient halés (tirés) par des chevaux.

Eine typische Schleuse aus dem neunzehnten Jahrhundert in dem Fluß Samme in Seneffe. Der Fluß wird von einem Treidelpfad flankiert, auf dem die Schiffe bis nach dem zweiten Weltkrieg von den Pferden getreidelt (gezogen) wurden.

Steengroeve in de omgeving
van Malmédy.

A quarry in the surroundings
of Malmédy.

Carrière dans les environs de
Malmédy.

Ein Steinbruch in der
Umgebung von Malmédy.

Deze gekloven landschappen
met open grotten of 'tiennes',
zoals de Fondry des Chiens,
zijn ontstaan door uitzetting
van het ijs in de prehistorie en
in eeuwen van erosie.
Ze maken deel uit van de rijke
variatie aan heuvels en
plateaus in het zuiden van het
land.

This cloven landscape with its
open caves or 'tiennes', like
the Fondry des Chiens, was
created by the expansion of
ice in prehistoric times
followed by centuries of
erosion. It is one of the rich
variety of hills and plateaux in
the southern part of the
country.

Ces paysages rongés, troués
de grottes ouvertes, ou
'tiennes', comme le Fondry
des Chiens, sont le fruit de la
dilatation de la glace durant la
préhistoire et de siècles
d'érosion. Ils font partie de la
grande diversité de collines et
plateaux du sud du pays.

Die zerklüfteten Landschaften
mit offenen, 'tiennes'
genannten Höhlen, wie die
'Fondry des Chiens',
entstanden durch die
Gletscher der Eiszeit und
Jahrhunderte andauernde
Erosion. Im Süden wechseln
Hügel und Hochebenen
einander ab.

In de Hoge Venen wordt een zeldzame keer nog turf gestoken, vroeger gebruikt als brandstof en nu als turfmolm voor bodembestrooiing in de tuinbouw.

In the Hautes Fagnes peat is still, although rarely, cut. It was formerly used as fuel and nowadays as peat dust for ground covering in horticultural activities.

A de rares occasions on extrait encore la tourbe dans les Hautes Fagnes, que l'on utilisait jadis comme combustible et qui de nos jours est une matière utilisée pour être répandue sur le sol dans l'horticulture.

Im Hohen Venn wird seltsamerweise noch Torf gestochen, der früher als Brennstoff und heute als Torfmull für die Bodenbedeckung im Gartenbau benutzt wird.

Het Zoniënwoud ligt op een boogscheut van het centrum van Brussel. Het is een oase van rust voor de wandelaars en gemakkelijk te bereiken via de Welriekende Dreef.

The Forêt de Soignes is a stone's throw away from the centre of Brussels. It is an oasis of peace for walkers and easy to reach via the 'Welriekende Dreef'.

A proximité du centre de Bruxelles, la forêt de Soignes est une oasis de tranquillité. Les promeneurs s'y rendent par la Drève de Bonne-Odeur.

Der 'Zonien'-Wald (Forêt de Soignes) ist nur einen Steinwurf von der Brüsseler Innenstadt entfernt. Er ist für Wanderer eine Oase der Ruhe und leicht zu erreichen via die 'Welriekende Dreef'.

De basiliek van Koekelberg van architect Albert van Huffel. Een mastodont sanctuarium dat vijftig jaar op zijn afwerking liet wachten en dat een van de referentie-punten in het Brusselse verkeer is.

La basilique de Koekelberg de l'architecte Albert van Huffel. Un sanctuaire énorme dont l'achèvement dura cinquante ans et qui est un des points de repère dans la circulation bruxelloise.

The Basilica of Koekelberg by architect Albert van Huffel. It took fifty years before this huge sanctuary was finally finished. It is one of the main landmarks in the traffic of Brussels.

Die Basilika von Koekelberg des Architekten Albert van Huffel. Ein Mastodon-Sanktuarium, das 50 Jahre auf seine Fertigstellung warten ließ und einen der Bezugs-punkte im Brüsseler Verkehr darstellt.

De Albert II-laan op loop-afstand van het Rogierplein. De voormalige Jacqmainlaan heeft door de aanwezigheid van een aantal miniwolken-krabbers (rechts ziet u de Belgacomtoren) een totaal nieuwe skyline gekregen.

L'avenue Albert II à deux pas de la place Rogier. L'ancienne avenue Jacqmain a obtenu une ligne des toits totalement neuve par la présence d'un certain nombre de gratte-ciel de basse altitude (à droite vous voyez la tour de Belgacom).

The Albert II-laan near the Rogierplein (Square Rogier). The former Jacqmainlaan received a completely new skyline because of the presence of a few small skyscrapers (on the right you can see the Belgacom Tower).

Die Albert-II-Laan im Bereich des Rogierplein. Die frühere Jacqmainlaan hat durch die Anwesenheit einer Reihe von Mini-Wolkenkratzern (rechts sehen Sie den Belgacom-Turm) eine vollständig neue Skyline bekommen.

Het hellend vlak van Ronquières. Het vlak is een hypergesofisticeerde sluis die een verval van 68 meter overbrugt. Twee schepen van elk 1.350 ton kunnen tegelijk in de tegenovergestelde richting versast worden in twee bakken van elk 91 meter.

Le plan incliné de Ronquières. Le plan est une écluse hyper-sophistiquée qui relie une différence de niveau d'eau de 68 mètres. Il est possible de sasser en même temps en sens contraire deux bateaux, pesant chacun 1.350 tonnes, dans deux bassins, mesurant chacun 91 mètres.

The sloping level of Ronquières. The level is a highly sophisticated sluice bridging a gap of 68 meters. Two ships of each 1.350 tons can simultaneously be locked through in opposite basins of each 91 meters.

Die schiefe Ebene von Ronquières. Diese Ebene ist eine hochkomplizierte Schleuse, die ein Gefälle von 68 Meter überbrückt. Zwei Schiffe mit je 1.350 Tonnen können zugleich in entgegengesetzter Richtung in zwei Trögen mit je 91 Meter Länge geschleust werden.

Het klaverblad van Groot-Bijgaarden. Het genie van de burgerlijke bouwkunde was in de jaren zeventig en tachtig op zijn hoogtepunt. De autosnelwegen tussen Parijs en Antwerpen, Oostende en Aachen kruisen elkaar hier in een kunstig vlechtwerk.

Le trèfle de Grand-Bigard. L'activité du génie civil était à son comble dans les années soixante-dix et quatre-vingt. Les autoroutes reliant Paris et Anvers, Ostende et Aix-la-Chapelle s'entrecroisent à cet endroit pour former des entrelacs artistiques.

The clover leaf of Groot-Bijgaarden. In the seventies and eighties the genius of civil engineering reached its peak. Here, the highways between Paris and Antwerp, Ostend and Aachen cross each other in an artful interlacement.

Das Kleeblatt von Groot-Bijgaarden. Die Pionierleistungen der Architektur befanden sich in den siebziger und achtziger Jahren auf ihren Höhepunkt. Die Autobahnen zwischen Paris und Antwerpen, Ostende und Aachen kreuzen sich hier in einem kunstvollen Geflecht.

De Botanique is een geheel van een botanische tuin en een serregebouw dat onder de Hollandse bezetting gebouwd werd in een mengeling van gehouwen steen, glas en ijzer. Het herbergt het cultuurcentrum van de Franstalige gemeenschap.

Le Botanique est un ensemble comprenant un jardin botanique et un bâtiment contenant une grande serre qui fut construit sous l'occupation hollandaise en mélangeant la pierre taillée, le verre et le fer. Il héberge le centre culturel de la Communauté française.

The Botanique is an ensemble of a botanic garden and a hothouse structure that was built during Dutch occupation; it is a mix of chopped rock, glass and iron. It contains the cultural centre of the French-speaking Community.

Der Botanique bildet eine Einheit aus einem botanischen Garten und einem Gewächshausbau, der unter der holländischen Besetzung aus einem Gemisch von behauenem Stein, Glas und Eisen gebaut wurde. Er beherbergt das Kulturzentrum der französischsprachigen Gemeinschaft.

Het gebouw van Old England, een voormalig warenhuis, dat na renovatie het Muziekinstrumentenmuseum geworden is. Het bruine art-nouveaugebouw leunt met zijn ijzer en glas aan tegen de classicistische pendant die deel uitmaakt van de frontgebouwen op het Koningsplein.

Le bâtiment de Old England – jadis un grand magasin – fut rénové pour y héberger le Musée des instruments de musique. Le bâtiment art nouveau construit avec beaucoup de fer et de verre se trouve à côté d'une demeure néo-classique de grandeur comparable. Les autres bâtiments de la place Royale sont également de style néo-classique.

The building of Old England, a former department store which was turned into the Musical instrument Museum after renovation. The brown Art Nouveau building with its iron and glass construction leans against the classicistic companion piece which forms part of the front building on the Koningsplein (The King's Square).

Das Gebäude von Old England, ein früheres Warenhaus, daß nach der Überholung das Musikinstrumentenmuseum geworden ist. Das braune Art Nouveau-Gebäude lehnt sich mit seinem Eisen und Glas an das klassizistische Gegenstück an, das einen Teil der Frontgebäude am Koningsplein bildet.

Het radiogebouw aan het Flageyplein van architect Joseph Diongre. Het gebouw, informeel de pakketboot genoemd, herbergde tot de jaren zeventig de BRT-radio en -televisie en krijgt nu na renovatie een culturele bestemming.

Le bâtiment de la radio place Flagey de l'architecte Joseph Diongre. Le bâtiment – familièrement appelé le paquebot – hébergeait jusque dans les années soixante la radio et télévision BRT; à présent il a une destination culturelle après rénovation.

The radio building at the Flageyplein (Square Flagey) by architect Joseph Diongre. The building, commonly called the packet boat, until the seventies contained the BRT (Belgian Radio and Television); now, after renovation, it has a cultural destination.

Das Rundfunkgebäude am Flageyplein des Architekten Joseph Diongre. Das Gebäude, gewöhnlich das Paketboot genannt, beherbergte bis in die siebziger Jahre den Rundfunk und das Fernsehen BRT und bekommt nun nach der Renovierung eine kulturelle Bestimmung.

Het Koninklijke Paleis in Brussel, werkresidentie van koning Albert II. De vlag op het gebouw geeft aan dat de koning in het land is. Op de achtergrond, van rechts naar links: het Justitiepaleis, het Hiltonhotel en een wolkenkrabber op de bolwerksquare aan de Naamsepoort.

Le Palais Royal à Bruxelles, résidence de travail du roi Albert II. Le drapeau en haut du bâtiment indique que le roi est dans le pays. A l'arrière-plan, de droite à gauche : le palais de Justice, l'hôtel Hilton et un gratte-ciel situé le long du square du boulevard porte de Namur.

The Royal Palace in Brussels, work residence of King Albert II. The flag shows that the King is in the country. At the background, from the right to the left: the Palace of Justice. The Hilton Hotel and a skyscraper on the Bolwerksquare (Bastion Square) at the Naamsepoort.

Das Koninklijke Paleis in Brüssel, die Arbeitsresidenz von König Albert-II. Die Flagge auf dem Gebäude zeigt an, daß der König im Lande ist. Im Hintergrund von rechts nach links: der Justizpalast, das Hilton-Hotel und ein Wolkenkratzer am Bolwerksquare am Naamsepoort.

De Warande (1787): een groene oase in het cementen hart van Brussel. De Oostenrijkse architect Bartholomeus Zinner traceerde het passersymbool van de loge in het grondplan van het park.

Le parc de Bruxelles(1787) : une oasis verte dans le cœur cimenté de Bruxelles. L'architecte autrichien Bartholomeus Zinner traça le symbole du compas de la loge dans le plan du parc.

The Warande (1787): a green oasis in the cement heart of Brussels. The Austrian architect Bartholomeus Zinner traced out the compass symbol of the lodge in the ground plan of the park.

De Warrande (1787): eine grüne Oase im Betonherz von Brüssel. Der österreichische Architekt Bartholomeus Zinner trassierte das Zirkelsymbol von der Loge in den Grundriß des Parks.

Een hoeve op een boogscheut van Brussel, net aan de overkant van de Grote Ring in Zellik. Een zicht van de hoofdstad vanuit Vlaanderen: achteraan rechts het Justitiepaleis.

A farmhouse near Brussels, just accross the Ring around Brussels in Zellik. A sight at the capital from Flanders: at the back on the right the Palace of Justice.

Une ferme non loin de Bruxelles, de l'autre côté du Grand Ring (périphérique) à Zellik. Une vue de la capitale au départ de la Flandre: à l'arrière à droite le palais de Justice.

Ein Gehöft, nur einen Steinwurf von Brüssel entfernt, genau gegenüber dem Grote Ring in Zellik. Ein Blick auf die Hauptstadt von Flandern aus: hinten rechts der Justizpalast.

Het Stocqletpaleis (1911) op de Brusselse Tervurenlaan. Het ontwerp van de Oostenrijkse architect Joseph Hoffmann maakte de overgang tussen de art nouveau en de modern style. Het is het meest unieke architecturale bouwwerk van Brussel.

Le palais Stocqlet (1911) situé le long de l'avenue de Tervuren bruxelloise. Le projet de l'architecte autrichien Joseph Hoffmann réalisa le passage de l'art nouveau au modern style. C'est la construction architecturale la plus originale de Bruxelles.

The Stocqlet Palace (1911) on the Tervurenlaan in Brussels. The design of the Austrian architect Joseph Hoffmann represents the transition period between the art nouveau and the modern style. It is Brussels' most unique architectural construction.

Das Stocqletpalais (1911) an der Brüsseler Tervurenlaan. Der Entwurf des österreichischen Architekten Joseph Hoffmann schuf den Übergang zwischen der Art Nouveau und dem modernen Stil. Es ist das einzigartigste Architekturbauwerk von Brüssel.

De kathedraal van Sint-Goedele en Sint-Michiel, de kathedraal waar de Belgische vorsten huwen en begraven worden. De hoofdkerk van Brussel wordt geflankeerd door de Nationale Bank en het administratieve gebouw van de Vlaamse Gemeenschap.

La cathédrale Saint-Michel et Gudule, la cathédrale où les souverains belges se marient et sont enterrés. L'église principale de Bruxelles est entourée par la Banque Nationale de Belgique et le bâtiment administratif de la Communauté flamande.

The cathedral of Saint-Goedele and Saint-Michiel, being the one where the Belgian monarchs get married and are buried. The main church of Brussels is flanked by the National Bank and the administrative building of the Flemish Community.

Die Kathedrale von Sint-Goedele und Sint-Michiel, die Kathedrale, in der die belgischen Fürsten getraut und begraben wurden. Die Hauptkirche von Brüssel wird flankiert von der Nationale Bank und dem Verwaltungsgebäude der flämischen Gemeinschaft.

Het Charlemagnegebouw aan de Brusselse Wetstraat, de vestigingsplaats van de Europese Commissie. Rechts een vleugel van het gereno- veerde Berlaimontgebouw en aan de overkant van de Wetstraat een stuk van het Residence Palace.

Le bâtiment le Charlemagne situé le long de la rue de la Loi bruxelloise, le lieu d'établisse- ment de la Commission européenne. A droite une aile du bâtiment Berlaimont et de l'autre côte de la rue de la Loi une partie du Résidence Palace.

The Charlemagne building in the Wetstraat in Brussels, the seat of the European Commission. On the right a wing of the renovated Berlaimont building and across the Wetstraat a part of the Residence Palace.

Das Charlemagne-Gebäude an der Brüsseler Wetstraat, dem Sitz der Europäischen Kommission. Rechts ein Flügel des renovierten Berlaimont- Gebäudes und gegenüber der Wetstraat ein Stück des Residenzpalasts.

Brussel is de hoofdstad van Europa, de Commissie heeft er haar zetel en administratie. Het Europees Parlement vergadert in dit majestueuze halfrond, de Espace Leopold, dat uittroont boven het Leopoldstation.

Bruxelles est la capitale de l'Europe. La Commission y a établi son siège et son administration. Le Parlement européen se réunit dans ce majestueux hémicycle, l'Espace Léopold, qui trône au-dessus de la gare du Quartier Léopold.

Brussels is the capital of Europe. The headquarters of the European Commission are situated in the city. The European Parliament sits at this majestic semi-circular building, the Espace Leopold, overlooking the Leopold Station.

Brüssel ist die Hauptstadt Europas. Die EU-Kommission hat hier ihren Sitz und ihre Verwaltung. Das Europäische Parlament tagt in diesem majestätischen Halbkreis, dem 'Espace Leopold', der den alten Leopoldbahnhof überragt.

Het NAVO-hoofdkwartier in Evere, zeg maar het Europese Pentagon. Hier is het beslissingscentrum en worden de vergaderingen gehouden van de Noord-Atlantische Verdragsorganisatie.

Le quartier général de l'Otan à Evere, on pourrait dire le Pentagone européen. Ici se trouve le centre de décision et se tiennent le réunions de l'Organisation du Traité de l'Atlantique Nord.

NATO-headquarters in Evere, say the European Pentagon, where the decision centre is situated and where the meetings of the North Atlantic Treaty Organisation are held.

Das NATO-Hauptquartier in Evere, sozusagen das europäische Pentagon. Hier ist das Entscheidungs- und Beratungszentrum der Organisation des Nordatlantikpakts.

Dit prachtige park werd aangelegd ter gelegenheid van de vijftigste verjaardag van het koninkrijk. Aan weerszijden van de triomfboog bevinden zich musea: aan de linkerkant het Legermuseum, aan de rechterkant het Museum voor Kunst en Geschiedenis en Autoworld. De Wetstraat loopt hier onder het park en de triomfboog door.

Ce parc magnifique a été dessiné à l'occasion du cinquantième anniversaire du royaume. Des musées flanquent les deux côtés de l'arc de triomphe: à gauche, le musée de l'Armée et, à droite, le musée d'Arts et d'Histoire ainsi qu'Autoworld. La rue de la Loi passe sous le parc et l'arc de triomphe.

This beautiful park was laid out to mark the fiftieth anniversary of Belgian independence. There are museums on either side of the triumphal arch. On the left is the Military Museum and on the right the Museum of Art and History and Autoworld. The 'Wetstraat' runs beneath the ark and the arch.

Diese prunkvolle Parkanlage wurde zum 50. Geburtstag des Königreiches eingeweiht. An beiden Seiten des Triumphbogens befinden sich Museen: links das Armeemuseum, rechts das Museum für Kunst und Geschichte, sowie die Sammlung 'Autoworld'. Unterirdisch verläuft die berühmte 'Wetstraat'.

De tentoonstellingsparken van de Brusselse Heizel beschikken over grote parkeerruimtes. Een close-up levert deze abstracte foto op.

Le parc des expositions, au Heysel, à Bruxelles, dispose de grands parkings. Un gros plan donne cette photo abstraite.

The Heysel Exhibition Centre in Brussels has large car parks. This abstract photograph is a close-up view.

Das Heyzel-Messegelände in Brüssel verfügt über riesige Parkplätze. Eine Nahaufnahme führte zu diesem abstrakten Bild.

Veiligheid, elektronica en techniek kunnen perfect samengaan met esthetiek, zoals deze sierlijke arabesken op de tarmac van de luchthaven van Zaventem bewijzen.

Sécurité, électronique et technique peuvent faire leur menage avec l'esthétique, ainsi que le prouvent ces gracieuses arabesques sur le tarmac de l'aéroport de Zaventem.

Safety, electronics and technology can go hand in hand with aesthetics, like these decorative arabesques on the tarmac at the airport of Zaventem.

Sicherheit, Elektronik und Technik vertragen sich offenbar bestens mit Ästhetik, wie diese eleganten Arabesken auf dem Runway des Flughafens Zaventem beweisen.

Het Brusselse beursgebouw zit ten troon op de Anspach-laan. De beeldhouwwerken op het fronton zijn van Rodin. Op de achtergrond ziet u enkele gevels van de Grote Markt.

Le bâtiment bruxellois de la Bourse 'trône' l'avenue Anspach. Les sculptures sur le fronton sont de Rodin. A l'arrière-plan vous voyez quelques façades de la Grand-Place.

The Brussels Bourse building, looking down on the Anspachlaan. The sculptures on the fronton are Rodin's. In the background you can see a few of the façades of the Grote Markt.

Das Brüsseler Börsengebäude thront auf der Anspachlaan. Die Bildhauerarbeiten am Fronton sind von Rodin. Im Hintergrund sehen Sie einige Fassaden des Grote Markt.

Het Brusselse stadhuis, een fraai voorbeeld van profane hoog-gotiek. Het werd gebouwd tussen 1402 en 1450 door Van Tienen en Dornay. De bouw van de lichtjes hellende toren werd in 1454 afgewerkt naar de plannen van architect Van Ruisbroek.

L'hôtel de ville de Bruxelles, un bel exemple de premier gothique profane. Le bâtiment fut construit entre 1402 et 1450 par Van Tienen et Dornay. La construction de la tour légèrement inclinée fut achevée d'après les plans de l'architecte Van Ruisbroek.

The Brussels city hall, a fine example of the secular High-Gothic style. It was built between 1402 and 1450 by van Tienen and Dornay. The construction of the slightly sloping tower was finished in 1454 according to the plans of architect Van Ruisbroek.

Das Brüsseler Rathaus, ein hübsches Beispiel der profanen Hochgotik. Es wurde zwischen 1402 und 1450 von Van Tienen und Dornay gebaut. Der Bau der leicht geneigten Turme wurde 1454 nach den Plänen des Architekten Van Ruisbroek fertiggestellt.

De Montgomerysquare op de Tervurenlaan. Recent werd er een fontein geïnstalleerd boven het gelijknamige metrostation. In de slagschaduw onderaan links staat het standbeeld.

The Montgomery Square at the Tervurenlaan. Recently a fountain has been installed above the subway station with the same name. In the cast shadow at the bottom on the left stands the statue.

Le Square Montgomery avenue de Tervuren. Récemment une fontaine a été installée au dessus de la station de métro qui porte le même nom.

Der Montgomery Square in der Tervurenlaan. Vor kurzem wurde ein Springbrunnen über der gleichnamigen Metrostation installiert. Im Schlagschatten unten links steht das Standbild.

Robberechts, Wim
Belgium, a View from the Sky

© 2007, Wim Robberechts en Uitgeverij Davidsfonds NV
Blijde-Inkomststraat 79-81, 3000 Leuven
Vormgeving en omslagontwerp: Geert Verstaen/Sin Aerts
Foto's: Wim Robberechts

D/2007/0240/43
ISBN: 978 90 5826 481 7

Belgium, the movie is een Engelstalige promotiefilm voor België. De film duurt 25 minuten en werd samengesteld door WIM ROBBERECHTS & CO, een productiehuis dat bedrijfsfilms en video's voor overheidsdiensten maakt. Het productiehuis heeft zich daarnaast gespecialiseerd in het maken van luchtopnamen vanuit een helikopter.
De film toont de geschiedenis van België aan de hand van luchtopnamen. Ook infrastructuur, economie, onderwijs en gezondheidszorg, landbouw en natuurbehoud komen aan bod.
Het is de allereerste film over België die in High Definition werd gedraaid.

Belgium, the movie est un film en anglais d'une durée de 25 minutes, qui est destiné à promouvoir la Belgique. Il est l'oeuvre de WIM ROBBERECHTS & CO, une société de production qui réalise des films d'entreprise et des vidéos pour des services publics. Cette société s'est également spécialisée dans les prises de vue aériennes par hélicoptère.
Le film retrace l'histoire de la Belgique vue du ciel. Il évoque aussi d'autres aspects tels que l'infrastructure, l'économie, l'enseignement, les soins de santé, l'agriculture et la préservation de la nature.
C'est le tout premier film sur la Belgique à avoir été tourné en Haute Définition.

Belgium, the movie is an English-language promotional film about Belgium. Its duration is 25 minutes and it was made by WIM ROBBERECHTS & CO, a production company that makes corporate films and videos for government departments. The production company has also specialized in aerial shots from a helicopter.
The film shows the history of Belgium on the basis of aerial shots. It deals with infrastructure, the economy, education, health care, agriculture and environmental conservation.
It is the first film about Belgium to be shot in High Definition.

Belgium, the movie ist ein englischsprachiger Werbefilm uber Belgien. Der Film dauert 25 Minuten und wurde vom Produktionshaus WIM ROBBERECHTS & CO angefertigt, ein Betrieb der v.a. gewerbliche Filme sowie Videos für Behörden erstellt. Das Produktionshaus hat sich außerdem auf Filmaufnahmen vom Hubschrauber aus spezialisiert. Der Film zeigt die Geschichte Belgiens anhand von Luftaufnahmen. Auch die Infrastruktur, Wirtschaft, Bildungs- und Gesundheitswesen, Landwirtschaft und Naturschutz werden behandelt.
Belgium, the movie ist der erste Film über Belgien, der in High Definition gedreht wurde.